BACK TO
THE BLACKBOARD

Design for a
Biblical Christian School

JAY E. ADAMS

A Book for Parents, Teachers, and Administrators

Presbyterian and Reformed Publishing Company
Phillipsburg, New Jersey 08865

ISBN 0-87552-075-8

PRINTED IN THE UNITED STATES OF AMERICA

To my grandchildren,
by whose time
there may be a
truly
Christian
education
available

CONTENTS

PREFACE

It was both easy and difficult to write this book. I have long dreamed over it, struggled over it, prayed over it and labored over it. Everything in it has been coming for a long time. When I finally sat down to write it, words and ideas gushed out. It was almost impossible to hold them back.

The fervor with which I wrote flowed from a very deep concern that is expressed in the first chapter. In one way or another, I have been in education most of my life. And I think I know the problems. While I have never taught regularly in a Christian day school, my children have attended Christian schools, and I have spoken at local and national school conventions across the country. I know a number of Christian teachers and parents with whom I have discussed these matters from time to time at length. I have agonized over what has been happening to my own children and those of parents whom I have tried to help both informally and in counseling. I think that I know just about all sides of the enterprise, from the inside out to the outside in.

I have focused on the Christian day school, rather than the college or the theological seminary, not because it is in worse shape but because I see there both the greatest opportunity for change and, at the same time, the most important area of education to confront now. Bible colleges and seminaries are likewise due for an overhaul. The principles that are discussed here apply to both with equal force. But as much as I should have cared to take on the task of proposing a new approach for those two sorts of institutions, I refrained from doing so for lack of time. Moreover, if a change of any size can be brought about in the Christian day schools, the students coming from such schools will themselves express their discontent with the humanistic methods and/or content of what they encounter. Strategically also (as you shall see from chapter 1), the Christian day school was the place to focus attention.

It is my hope that many parents, teachers and administrators will become sufficiently aroused by this book to do something concrete about the situation that exists in their schools. It is too late for my own children to profit from any change, but perhaps my grandchildren will be the heirs to a new and exciting education that at once honors Jesus Christ and enables children to do so too. If they are not, they may be in prison.

Jay E. Adams
The Millhouse
1981

1

THE NEED

Perhaps at no other moment in American history has there been so great a need as at the present for a strong, viable witness for Christ.

I know that Christians have been saying that sort of thing down through history. Indeed, we are so used to reading such statements that they no longer make much of an impression upon us. That, in itself, is one important danger sign. But there are some special reasons for viewing the present time as a peculiarly critical period upon which long stretches of the future may hang in the balance. Depending on how you and I meet the need about which I shall speak, our children and our children's children may live in an age of unprecedented darkness, violence, persecution and chaos, or in an era of unparalleled peace and spiritual prosperity.

For some time now, Western culture has been deteriorating at a frightening rate. Values, norms, and order all have been thrown into the air. The slaughter of 1.5 million unborn babies each year; the struggle to ward off the libertarian emphases in the ERA movement; the skirmishes that the Christian school movement has had with the IRS; the widespread acceptance of homosexuality and hard-core pornography in movies, at the newsstand, on HBO and home video cassettes; the mounting divorce rate among Christians, as well as in the general public; the drug culture and a host of similar indicators, all too familiar to bore you with, make it clear that in this year in which I write (1980) something definitive is about to happen.

Warnings and preliminary judgments of an economic and political nature, mercifully visited on the nation, have gone unheeded. Many of our leaders in every sphere of life seem bent on destroying all that in the past has been held sacred and valuable and on wiping it from our memories forever.

Humanism is rampant. Everywhere in a society that for over a generation has been almost totally feeling oriented ("If it feels good, do it"), hedonistic humanism prevails. Man is the measure of all things. And

1

what is most important about man is how he feels. Current humanism is not a virile humanism that conceives of man as a heroic, courageous, bold, self-sufficient and self-sacrificing superman; rather, it tends to cultivate the type of person who becomes a cloying, pampered, spoiled brat, the inevitable result of a generation of self-centered advertising, unchecked immorality and wide-open pleasure seeking. Modern man is suffering from the never-satisfying, but ever-intoxicating, disease of human voluptuousness. He is determined to gratify his sensual and sensuous desires, satiating himself with as much gusto as possible because "you only go 'round once." In short, because he denies, ignores or doesn't know the relevance of the cross and resurrection of Jesus Christ, because he has been taught that man is an animal with no more future life than an ant, he has pursued ruthlessly the logical consequence of the philosophy Paul articulated so clearly long ago, the quest for pleasure *now:* "If the dead aren't raised, let us eat and drink; tomorrow we die" (I Cor. 15:32b).

About such a society God makes this pronouncement: "Those who practice such things deserve death." As Paul astutely observes: "They not only do them, but heartily approve of those who practice them" (Rom. 1:32). That is the way God looks at the society in which we live.

We must not think, however, of our society as a generation of passive sops, dandies who revel in silks and satins, who care more for manners and mores than for morals. No, it is exactly not that. Today's society lacks all the refinement and taste; like any other spoiled child on whom so much has been lavished and from whom so little has been required, it is an uncouth, demanding one that shows absolutely no gratitude to the persons and the institutions from which it received all its comforts and advantages. It is an unsettled, seeking-but-never-finding, changeable, volatile society, ready to try anything but satisfied with nothing. It will shove anyone out of the way to be first in line and, like a confused animal, will turn quickly on those who are most concerned to help alleviate its miseries. It is unpredictable, dangerous and self-destructive.

In the midst of such a culture (using that word in a neutral rather than a positive sense) what can a Christian do? What is his place? Where does he begin? And, of most importance to the reader of this book, what part can (must) Christian education play in determining the future?

Fuller answers to those questions must be given in the chapters that follow; for now, I wish to focus on but one: Christians, and in particular

2

Christian educators, must learn to read the "signs of the times."

When Jesus rebuked the crowds it was not for failure to heed some sort of special revelation about the day in which they lived (though, of course, they should have been able to discern from the constellation of Old Testament prophecies coverging upon their day that it was the time for a first messianic coming). Rather, He rebuked them for not being able to "interpret" the times from the events they were experiencing day by day. He said, "When you see a cloud rising in the west, right away you say, 'A storm is coming,' and it does. And when you see a south wind blowing you say, 'It's going to be hot,' and it is. You hypocrites! You know how to interpret the appearance of the earth and the sky, but why is it that you don't know how to interpret the present time?" (Luke 12:54b-56).

The analogy is clear. He points out to them that when they see "signs" (indicators) of approaching changes in the weather, from them they are able to predict accurately (note, "and it does," "and it is") the coming of a storm, a hot spell, etc. Then, He asks, in effect, "If you can reason correctly about the weather from the many indications that you see all around you, why haven't you been able to reason out what is taking place?" It did not take a prophet to figure out the signs of the times. Nor does it today.

I make no claims to be a prophet; I have no direct pipeline through which to obtain extrabiblical revelation. But it doesn't take a gift of prophecy to read the signs of our times. They are as obvious as a storm cloud "rising in the west." Yet, it seems to me that all too few Christians are looking at the sky (most are too much occupied with earthly things). Let me tell you how I read these signs.

First of all, I have already described the galloping humanism that has all but taken over educational, political and social institutions. At no time in American history has there been such an aggressive, powerful, out-front, assertive, and persuasive anti-Christian force. Any attempt to overthrow it meets the most formidable resistance. It has knocked out one contender after another until there is no opponent left but the church of the Lord Jesus Christ.

That fact leads to a second. There is another set of signs that are often missed by Christians. But they ought to be apparent to anyone who even casually has watched the course of Bible-believing Christianity over the past 25 years. During that time, if he stepped outside at all, an observant

Christian could not fail to sense the shift of the prevailing winds. The cold, arctic blasts of liberalism that once howled unmercifully have, after a few final gusts, given way to the softer breezes of warm evangelical truth.

Indeed, from nearly every indicator that we may wish to consult, including numerical and economic figures, it is clear that while the evil one has been successfully promoting humanism in the land, the Lord also has been quietly but actively rebuilding His true church. Never before has humanism had so strong an upper hand, it is true; but it is just as true that there has never been a time in the history of American Christianity that the church has had so many members, so much money, so many resources, such potentially powerful institutions, such a grasp on the media. And, among these, standing out in the clearest profile is the Christian school movement. With its enormous capacity for growth, it is now sending out shoots in every direction, like a very healthy kudzu vine. In the minds of many it may be the most potently packed prospect of all.

There are giants abroad in the land! And, unless my eyes deceive me, we can offer a prediction that is just about as certain as tonight's weather. It is this: these two giants, secular humanism and evangelical Christianity, are squaring off for the battle of the century, perhaps the battle *for* the century to come.

Surely God has not given the church all the resources she now possesses merely for her comfort and pleasure. She will need them, and need them all, in the coming conflict. And, from the vastness of the supplies now being stockpiled, it would seem that the war will be long and hard fought.

Of course, the winds could change abruptly, and all my predictions fail. But if the clouds now gathering in the sky mean anything, we would be wise to prepare for a storm. Already we have felt some drops of rain. There have been some early confrontations between these giants, who have been sparring outside the ring. But when the bell sounds and they come out of their corners, it will be in earnest, and the church will know at last that she is in a win or lose situation. There is much to be won or lost, and there will be no TKOs or winning on points. One opponent or the other will be knocked flat before it is all over.

The need, therefore, is for preparation. Each of us must understand his task, know how to go to the final round if necessary, and know how to come out on top. How will the church prepare herself, and whom will she put into the ring?

By the year 2000, and perhaps sometime before, it should no longer be news who won the fight. The time is short, preparation must be intense. Chief among those who will find themselves in the ring are many choice, young Christians who are now in Christian schools. Much of the coming battle will fall on their shoulders. They are unaware of the evil that portends their future, as are most Christian parents and teachers. But pastor, Christian teacher, parent, leader, whoever you are, wake up! The conflict is at hand. There is so little time left to ready the church for the great effort she must make. And there is so much to do. What is your part in the present task of preparation? Is it not to do all that you can to be sure that those young people are trained as well as possible?

That is what this book is all about, how to teach youth. I am convinced that the present training received in Christian schools is inadequate and will not see our youth through the days to come. I fear for them, for the land and for the church. Read carefully the proposal that I am about to make, which, if adopted, could reverse what I believe to be a desperate situation.

2

THE OPPORTUNITY

The coming conflict provides us with an unparalleled opportunity; that is how we must view it. We must neither shy away from the war that lies ahead nor crawl into holes along with certain well-meaning but misguided survivalists. Rather, we must be ready to meet the opponent in his own corner, carrying the fight to him.

The greatest opportunity that I know for spreading the gospel to the length and the breadth of this land and carrying the good news throughout the world in an unprecedented way during the next few years lies just ahead. If the church can defeat the humanistic giant, at the zenith of his powers, crippling him with decisive blows until there is no fight left in him, even greater resources will be available for such positive purposes as evangelism, and many wider opportunities for service will open. Seizing the opportunity, however, will require a concerted effort, and probably a very bruising battle. Humanism, having so fully triumphed, isn't likely to disappear on its own; it will have to be driven away by a force better trained and more powerful than itself.

The one area in which humanism has been most successful in gaining converts and in propagating its views has been in education—especially (but not exclusively, as we shall see later on) in the public school system. Allied with humanistic Supreme Court rulings, this system has been purging itself of every vestige of Christian teaching, ethics and morality. In turn, the public school has championed every standard humanistic objective and every sort of humanistic program. There can be no doubt in the mind of a wide-awake Christian who takes the time to investigate the evidence, that public schools (along with most state and private colleges and universities) form the fountainhead of humanistic propaganda and training in our society. If we are to defeat humanism, we must destroy it at the source—in the schools.

But the fact is that humanism in public education has failed. Never, in the history of the country, has so much money been dumped into any system with so few positive results. Not only can't Johnny read, but what he has learned to read has torpedoed his moral and ethical values and

6

turned him into a confused, sex-oriented, muddle-headed kid who possesses all sorts of facts he doesn't know what to do with. He can't make educational shish kebab out of his bits-and-pieces learning because humanism has taken away God as his integrative skewer.

In order to "liberate" him from the "chains" of traditional, biblical Christianity, humanism has taught the modern student to question everything and to accept nothing. He has learned to reject authority in the name of "scientific objectivity." Absolutes (except, of course, for the absolute pronouncements of humanism) are scrapped in favor of relativism; truth is debunked and replaced by the pragmatic, the utilitarian, and the operational.

But this humanistic teaching has backfired. Students, more consistently than their humanistic mentors, have been questioning and doubting even humanistic premises and practices. All this has led to the anarchy that prevails in modern education.

Alongside all of this, God has been raising up the Christian school movement. Rapidly, across the land, Christian schools have begun to multiply in an attempt to free children from the tentacles of the humanistic educational octopus. Probably there has been no more outstanding innovation among Christians in this generation than the Christian school movement. Nowhere is there a greater opportunity for combatting humanism than in education. Education has been the citadel of humanism. Now, in the Christian school, God has placed in our hands a marvelous power that can change all that.

Christian education is growing in numbers, in power, in resources and even in wealth. Indeed, it has become big business, as the booths at any ACSI convention give ample evidence. There is great opportunity, therefore, for training a large number of young people in alternative ways of thinking and living through educational programs firmly founded on Christian presuppositions and practices. If we can raise up a well-educated, capable, articulate and keen generation of outspoken and outstanding Christians who will excel in every field of endeavor, we shall capture those fields for Christ. A large number of such students poured out of Christian schools across the country could defeat humanism on every front.

The contrast between Christian students who succeed in grappling with the problems of a sinful world and those from pagan schools who cannot, could—above all else—make Christianity very attractive to the many who are baffled by the contradictory and nihilistic theses of humanism which, while promising to exalt and free man, in actual practice debase and enslave him. These anarchistic results have disillusioned many, who have lost faith in all education because they see no viable educational alternative to this system, which is obviously a failure.

But, in order to provide an alternative, in order to turn the tide, Christians must *demonstrate* that the product of Christian education is, in all respects, superior. Disillusioned humanists will not willingly listen to more claims that cannot be supported by performance. And that is just the rub—now, at the time when the opportunity is ripe, we fail to demonstrate it; the Christian school is not doing its job.

3

THE PROBLEM

So far, the Christian school has not demonstrably proved itself to be significantly superior to the public school. We do not see the impact that we should expect to see and that was predicted and hoped for 25 years ago. Why hasn't that happened?

You may say that it is yet too early to look for such results. That is not true; I think it is only an excuse. We already have many "second generation" teachers in Christian schools who themselves are the products of Christian schools. There are two large international associations of Christian schools, and a third that is rapidly growing. The number of students now in Christian education runs into the millions. By now many of the contrasts ought to be evident. But they aren't.

Instead, as I talk to Christian teachers and administrators all over the country, I find them to be dedicated, disillusioned and disappointed. They entered Christian education with great enthusiasm and large expectations; but both have been dampened. Perhaps you will say that they anticipated too much; their expectations were unrealistic. I disagree. The opportunities lying before Christian educators are vast, and the vision that many have had (and a great many still have) is more than realistic— it is, as I hope you will come to see, pitifully small. It will become clearer as you continue reading that the problem lies right there: there has been too little vision in the Christian school movement. It has settled for too little too soon. Many in the movement have rightly made great claims about what Christian education could do, and this has aroused the expectations of parents (who also are becoming more and more disillusioned—after all, they pay the bills added to their tax dollars, and should demand that the promises made be fulfilled), teachers and adminstrators who are devoting their lives to something they believe in. This belief is genuine; it is often accompanied by the ready acceptance of reductions in earnings and other benefits when compared to what they would receive from teaching in the public school. No wonder, then, that both parents and teachers want a change, something better, something significantly different from what they can find down the street. And they are entitled to it. Christian education should not only be different from pagan education—it can be. But why isn't it? Again, I answer, because of lack of vision.

Before I go any further, however, let me make it clear that I find both parents and teachers thankful for what differences they do already enjoy in most Christian schools. There are the joys of Christian fellowship among teachers, the opportunities to pray, to read the Bible and to talk about Christ, the lower rate of drug use and, usually (though not always), the better discipline. In fact, more than one parent or teacher will tell you that this is why he is a part of the movement. Possibly more children are sent to Christian schools for such reasons (not necessarily bad reasons, you understand) than for obtaining a distinctively Christian education.

But there is the point. Why is it that parents don't make a distinctively Christian education their first concern? Why is it that the greatest complaint I hear from Christian teachers is that they don't know how to teach in a distinctively Christian manner and are most disappointed when they recognize that, apart from the facts mentioned in the preceding paragraph, what they are doing is not appreciably different from what goes on at the pagan school down the street? And why is it that students graduating from Christian schools do not make a greater impact for Christ on their communities, at their jobs and in their churches? Why is it that among them there is so often an ''if-this-is-Christian-education-so-what?'' attitude rather than a recognition that they are involved in something very special, uniquely preparing them to assume roles in this world for Jesus Christ? Why do you so seldom meet a graduate of a Christian school who has a sense of destiny? In short, why aren't teachers, administrators, and parents *excited* about Christian education? The fact of lethargy in the church, so widely complained about among Christians in general, does not adequately answer the question. It only offers an excuse to those who are looking for one. Actually, it sharpens the basic question: why hasn't the Christian school become a powerful antidote to this lethargy? All admit that it has the potential to be such.

Again, I must answer all of these questions with one response: It is because of a lack of vision—the lack of a truly biblical vision—that there is so little excitement in Christian education.

Now it is about that lack of vision, about both its causes and cures, that this book has been written, with the hope that something constructive can be done to sweep aside the thickening professionalism that has been settling in on Christian education like a chilling fog in lieu of a sense of genuine adventure and excitement. The cutting-edge mentality with which Christian education began was dulled to that of a butter knife in very short order. Can it be honed up razor sharp again?

I am convinced that there not only can be but that there will be exciting times ahead; the Christian school has hardly even begun to realize its potential. But these times will not arrive until we catch the vision and follow it through the many difficult and, admittedly, precarious paths into which it will lead us. It is my hope that in this book I shall capture and accurately portray something of that vision for you, and that by it I shall be able to point you in the direction toward which it leads.

"But, more specifically, can you tell us what the problem is? Why aren't Christian schools excitingly different in every way? You have vaguely alluded to a 'lack of vision' and a 'lack of biblical vision,' but what do you mean by that?"

To begin to give you a clearer understanding of what I am getting at, in one sense, will take the whole book. But in the next chapter I shall try to pinpoint the principal problem that lies behind everything.

4

PEDDLING THE ENEMY'S PRODUCT

I have pictured the church and humanism squared off for a decisive battle in the near future. I have maintained that it will be crucial and that the outcome may well affect many generations to come. I have also suggested that the Christian school is one of the principal forces that must be marshalled for this conflict. And I have implied that at the present time neither the church nor the Christian school is prepared to do battle. Moreover, I have asserted that there is a growing discontent among parents and teachers alike with the practices and the results of Christian education as it is currently known, and I have hinted that something can be done about it if we catch and pursue a more biblical vision of Christian education. At the close of the previous chapter, I was asking why we haven't succeeded in producing an exciting alternative to the pagan school down the block, and I promised to tell you why. That is my concern in this chapter.

The problem, as I see it, can be stated quite simply: the Christian church in general, and the Christian school in particular, itself has been so heavily drenched with humanism that it is unable to create a viable alternative. This charge may take you by surprise, but, even on the surface of things, why should it? Isn't the history of the Old Testament a history of God's people becoming one in thought and practice with the nations around them until God brings them back to the right path again and again? In the New Testament, probably half of the books were written to counter similar tendencies in the infant church. Church history since has been a repeat performance. Why then should we be startled at the suggestion that it has happened once more?

It is true that the Christian school movement sees dimly the vision of truly biblical education, talks about it, yearns for it, tries to realize it; but it never seems to succeed in doing so. That is why I have great hope; it is not a case of apostasy, as so often it was when the people of Israel deliberately cast off Jehovah and turned to another god, but it is a case of unwitting collaboration, while wanting the very opposite. Christian educators are unaware of the fact that, in almost every essential, Christian education as it is currently practiced is based on humanistic pre-suppositions, works toward humanistic goals and follows humanistic practices.

Of course, there are a number of variations, and my sweeping statements, though accurately describing the situation as a whole, may be unfair if applied to particular schools. They must not be taken absolutely.

In my opinion, humanism is not only an external foe, but has become firmly entrenched in our ranks. Unaware of the great inroads of humanism, and with all of the best intentions, Christian schools have been attempting to do the impossible—they have been trying to create an alternative to humanism by offering more of the same. It is not possible to pursue humanistic goals by humanistic ways and means, and to end up with less rather than more humanism. Unwittingly humanistic principles are being propagated and practiced—perhaps even more successfully than by humanists themselves—by the very persons who want to counter them. It is my studied conviction that the Christian school movement is presently unable to achieve its deepest ends and lacks verve and excitement precisely because it is riddled with humanism. It is impossible to counter and cure a case of poisoning by administering larger and even more powerful doses of the same poison.

Because I have spoken so frequently about humanism, and because an understanding of it will play such an important part in all that I have to say, let me take time here to identify this subtle force a little more clearly. What is humanism?

Humanism is a world view, or philosophy of life, that in one way or another divorces God from His universe. Humanism considers man the measure and end of all things. Because in humanism man's happiness is the goal of life, feelings become all-important. It is in every way sensuous, feeling-oriented, hedonistic. Desires are relabeled "needs," and it is thought that human comfort and convenience must be achieved at all costs—even (inconsistently) at the cost of lives of millions of unborn babies. If there is any hope for the world, it must be found in human achievement; all change, all advance is brought about by man, for man. God, if He exists at all, (as Whitehead once put it) is "not available for religious purposes." Prayer is a futile exercise; if you want something done, you will have to do it for yourself. In short, humanism is man-centered paganism.

Now, does it seem likely that a movement that has as its avowed purpose to put God at the center of all things (as does the Christian school movement) would fall into the error of propagating and practicing humanism? Hardly, on the face of things. And yet, that is precisely what I believe it has done. That is why the cutting edge is missing. It is precisely because it sounds so preposterous to say so that the fact is not more apparent.

The befuddlement and growing dissatisfaction found among so many who are a part of the Christian school movement testify to the existence of some major difficulty. From where I sit—as an educator, as a parent who has had four children in Christian schools, in Christian colleges and in a Christian theological seminary, and as a frequent speaker at Christian school functions—I think that I see very plainly what is wrong. Christian education has been like a farmer who, wishing to kill the weeds in a field, sprays that field with nutrients that make them grow all the more, and then wonders what is wrong. It is not that he does so purposely, you must understand; he thinks that the spray he uses will kill the weeds. But that is where the whole problem arises—wishful thinking will not transform the spray into a herbicide. He has the right ultimate objective in mind, but he only frustrates his own purposes by continuing to do what he is doing. Someone must tell him where he is going wrong, or he will continue to propagate weeds. Not every farmer, in spite of the problem, would appreciate being told, I recognize.

Even the most casual survey of the modern history of Christian education shows plainly that Christian schools, on all levels, are little more than adaptations of pagan schools. These pagan schools are built and operated on humanistic presuppositions and principles for humanistic ends. With very little change, most of the presuppositions, goals, curricula, subject areas, materials and methods have been brought over into Christian education and "Christianized." The trouble is that a system that in all of its essentials is still fundamentally pagan and opposed to everything biblical cannot be transformed by Christianizing it. Adding Christian accouterments—a Christian faculty and administration, prayer, Bible reading, a Bible course or two, Christian slogans ("All truth is God's truth," "We must learn math for God's glory," and the like)—will not transform pagan education into Christian education. We have tried it—and failed. That is why Christians, connected in one way or another with Christian schools, are so frustrated; they know that it doesn't work. But they don't know what they are doing wrong. They are

14

like the farmer trying to fight weeds: the more effort they expend, the worse the problem. What then must be done to rectify the situation? And will Christian educators listen?

What Christian schools must do now is what they did not take the time to do at their inception: they must reexamine the basics of Christian education *biblically*. For whatever reasons, we were in a hurry. We didn't realize the magnitude of the task; we were led astray; those who pioneered Christian education were not exegetically and theologically adept; or there may have been other reasons. But the fact is that Christian schools got off on the wrong foot. As the result, even today, we lack a biblical vision of what Christian education could and should be.

The biblical vision that is lacking is not some vague, general, noble goal, already accessible to all Christians, if they would only take it; rather, it is composed of many biblical presuppositions, precepts and practices that must be mined at hard labor, smelted in the fires of repentance, and hammered out into a system under prayerful care and attention. We must become serious about Christian educational theory and practice; serious enough to reexamine everything that is currently being done in our schools. And by everything, I mean *everything,* down to the practice of eating lunch at school! We must go back to scratch, indeed, even further back—to itch!

I know change will not be easy to achieve, now that Christian education has become a smoothly working, skillfully operated success in many other ways. Indeed, as I have already had occasion to observe, it is big business. There will be opposition to change. Not everyone likes change in general, and when they read some of the radical, biblical proposals I shall make in this book, many more will dislike those changes in particular. Such proposals will especially disturb those with vested interests. But that must not deter us. Too much hangs on the matter of change to allow such opposition to frighten us off the platform. There is a great need, very soon, for a new breed of Christian school graduates to fight the coming battle. With that threat hanging over our heads, we must press forward as rapidly as possible, while at the same time taking care not to repeat the former error of moving too quickly to explore thoroughly all of the basics. We must learn to ask those questions that will lead more concretely to a detailed portrayal of the vision.

What, for instance, are the biblical presuppositions about the purposes of education as they relate to life and godliness? How should teaching be done? Whom shall we teach? What place does regeneration have in the learning process? These, and questions like them, must be answered before we can move ahead. Apart from clear, biblical answers to them, everything else in the Christian educational enterprise will go askew—as indeed it has. All else is conditioned by answers to such fundamental questions. That is why they can be ignored no longer.

Consider the following questions for a moment. Who should be accepted into the Christian school? Should Christian education be restricted to believers or to the children of believers? And is it to be for all such, or only for those who are intellectually capable of going to college? What does the raw product of Christian education look like?

The fact that the student is a sinner, for example, has sweeping implications about truth and error as well as morality and transgressions, which educators ought to explore. How does a teacher cope with problems of truth that grow out of sinful patterns rather than out of ignorance? Is teaching an intellectual enterprise only, or does it have a distinctively moral side? How does the fact of sin in the student's life affect teaching methodology?

Many other such questions might be asked, but even from this brief discussion you can see, can't you, that there is a lot of work to be done. In this book I have tried to do some of that work for you, but it will take far more than the efforts of one person in one book to complete the total task.

The pagan schools know nothing of this important insight into life, and therefore do not (cannot) take sin into account. All that they do, then, is predicated on a false view of man; they have failed to come to grips with the student as he really is. The Christian school must study every facet of this question, including every implication of sin for education. That will be pioneering work for the most part. The public school can contribute nothing to it.

When American schools became too sophisticated to publish the *New England Primer* (or a modern equivalent to it), with its dual purpose of instructing a child "in his duty" as well as encouraging him "in his learning," such great truths as "In *Adam's* fall we sinned all" disappeared from education altogether. Now, in public school neither teacher nor student takes any cognizance of the fact of sin from one classroom day to another. Christian educators must begin to do so. In adopting the basic system of the pagan schools, they also took over its lack of concerns and its omissions, along with everything else. That is why the great body of educational writing on the subject of sin and education by Christians, which you would expect to find, does not exist.

Clearly allied to the doctrine of sin, with all of its educational ramifications, is the all-important distinction between a regenerate and an unregenerate student. This distinction comes into play all across the board because the responses to Christian approaches to life by the regenerate, who have the ability to respond positively to God and to His truth, will necessarily be different from those of the unregenerate (I Cor. 2; Rom. 8:8). This distinction is of importance educationally because Christian education is dealing with truth. Can unregenerate students be required to have insights and live according to lifestyles that are impossible for them? Should the school's expectations, purposes, methods, and content be the same for both the regenerate and the unregenerate student? Or should there be some accommodation? Two tracks? And, by the way, how should a Christian school distinguish between who is and who is not regenerate?

Until there are plain answers to these questions and dozens of other questions like them, how can Christian education truly be Christian? The teaching of the Bible on every subject must be fully considered in relationship to all Christian teaching. Moreover, methods appropriate to biblical findings concerning these matters must be developed, tested and carefully refined. In our borrowing from pagan, humanistic, man-centered education, the structures and the methods that we adopted were built on assumptions that man is essentially good, fully capable of charting a proper course for himself, and entirely educable by intellectual means apart from regeneration and forgiveness.

A look at the Bible reveals the falsity of every one of these pagan dogmas. And note well, even though public schools do not think their educational system is based on doctrine, it is dogma nonetheless that they espouse. It may be bad doctrine; but that in no way diminshes the fact that a theology—good or bad—lies at the heart of everything done in education. Since this is true, Christians

(1) can never adopt precepts, principles or practices uncritically,

(2) must be sure they know doctrine well enough to make accurate critical judgments about what is done,

(3) and must be able to develop biblical approaches founded on true doctrine.

That means that Christian theorists, administrators, teachers and parents must become thoroughly acquainted with biblical teaching and adept at using Christian doctrine in the determination of what is done in Christian schools. Both the church and the school have failed to teach how to use biblical truth practically in everyday affairs and for planning and decision making. As the consequence, a host of problems has arisen.

It is essential for the Christian school movement to make an alliance, therefore, with concerned, capable Christian exegetes and theologians who can provide what is needed. No longer may it continue along its present course, ignorant of the implications of doctrine for teaching. About that I should like to say a few words in the chapter that follows.

5

WHERE DO WE GO FROM HERE?

In the previous chapter I tried to show how important doctrine is for any rebuilding of Christian education along new lines and for setting it once-and-for-all on a solidly biblical base. In doing so, as an example, I mentioned (but did not develop) the doctrines of sin and inability and noted that these doctrines have far-ranging implications for education. I shall discuss them further at a later point. Similarly, all other loci of doctrine also bear directly on Christian education—the doctrines of Scripture, God, creation, providence, man, sin, salvation, sanctification, the church, and the future. All of these areas, with all of their sub-topics, must be thoroughly examined.

It is my contention that we have not discovered the implications of doctrine for education largely because there have not been enough persons in the forefront of Christian education who possess (or at least have used) adequate exegetical and doctrinal ability to get the job done. Outside help will be needed. Many Christian school professionals have a doctorate in education or some allied subject, but little more than a Sunday school or (at best) a Bible college education in some biblical studies. That is why outside help will be needed.

But to call on and listen to others who are not directly a part of the Christian school movement will require humility from leaders in the movement and a willingness to sponsor innovation whenever they see a biblical necessity to do so. This will not come easily; some will resist change, calling it "theological meddling" or something of the sort. Fortunately, I have had the opportunity to meet some of the top leaders in Christian education in the past few years, and to a man I find them to be humble, teachable individuals who really care to be biblical. My deepest concerns are about others further down the line.

But pride, vested interests, inertia or any other obstacles that may be encountered must not be allowed to stand in the way of biblical change. The signs of the times, with their clear indications of impending storms, must be remembered. This is not a time for fearful insular, reactive thinking.

On the other hand, the enlistment of outside help must be done with great care. Persons must be selected who will truly help, and not hinder. Not all, probably not most, Christian theologians and exegetes themselves will prove helpful in the review and reworking of Christian education (though proper use of many of their writings will). Many of these men, who are technically proficient in their fields, lack just the sort of insight and ability that is needed to show others how to use biblical truth in practical situations. Their own methods are often stained the same color as the building we want to repaint. These modern day Erasmuses themselves are the product and very often the proponents of the very sorts of practices that I have described as the unwitting application of humanism in teaching. They are the academes of the first water. Stay away from all such!

While this book cannot undertake the entire task of outlining what a biblical renovation of Christian education will require, who might best effect it, and how it might proceed, I do hope to chart enough of a course, set forth enough guidelines, and do enough exegetical and theological work to indicate clearly what must be done. In my opinion, however, a small, carefully selected group of theological and educational leaders, adequately funded by the Christian school movement, or others meeting together periodically over a period of five or six years, might be able to do the thorough sort of job that is required.

But that is not to say that an individual school, or school system, itself could not begin right away to make sound, basic alterations along the lines of what they will find in this book. Some have taken first steps toward doing so. The proposals are complete enough to help any school get under way. And it is my hope that there will be many more schools and even many teachers who, reading this book, will begin to make changes, partial though they may be at first, that will move Christian education significantly closer to the biblical ideals she has espoused but so far has not attained.

In the meantime, if such a select gathering of educators and theologians could be properly financed and enlisted, greater progress than we have yet dreamed about could be reached speedily. Here is where a Christian businessman, entrepreneur, a syndicate of the same or a foundation could profitably invest a one-time gift of money that might have lasting impact on the future of Christianity in America in a very significant way. I can think of few investments that might bring greater spiritual returns. If the vision takes on reality as you read, and you would like to consider this matter further, I should be glad to discuss it in depth and put you in touch with some educators that I believe might also be interested.

The study that such a commission undertakes, like the principles that it follows, should not be done academically, but should be done practically, in conjunction with one or more Christian schools with which it will work in actually testing, demonstrating and teaching its findings. It must become a discipling body that produces a functioning program of Christian education. To do so, there will need to be Christian schools open to having such a program instituted at least on a pilot level. These, too, may contact me.

But such a commission does not exist and may never come into existence. What, then, can a local school or teacher with vision, who is in a position of some flexibility, do? Much, to which the rest of the book is devoted.

6

THE PURPOSES OF EDUCATION

I have charged that the Christian school movement unintentionally has taken over humanistic goals from its secular counterpart. Pagan purposes, of course, are not well defined or agreed on by all. That is why, similarly, if you lasso the first 12 teachers you meet at the next Christian school convention and ask them, "What are the purposes of Christian education?" you will probably get 12 different answers. Pagan confusion about what we ought to be doing has been imported along with everything else. We are educating, but we don't know why. Think of it!

What are the purposes of Christian education, then? How are we going to determine what they are? We shall find it necessary to turn to the Scriptures in a new and fresh way to discover what God has to say about the matter.

THE GLORY OF GOD

Of course, the one overall goal that we must set for everything we do is the glory of God. But to say that in the way so many of those who attempt to teach in a Christian manner do is to denude it of all meaning. It is time that we stopped glibly repeating words that amount to little more than an ill-understood slogan. Those words, "All right, children; let's do our math (or whatever) for the glory of God," provide no magic formula that will transform an otherwise humanistic course of study, or school activity, into *Christian* education. These words must not be tacked onto pagan thought and action the way they so often have been. Ordinarily, they have little or no meaning, but at best they disguise the true humanistic nature of what is actually happening. Humanism cannot be converted into Christianity by uttering some Christian "Open sesame."

Well, if the glory of God is to be the over-arching goal of all that a Christian does, what does it mean to do something "for God's glory"?

Until you can answer that question definitively you will get nowhere. On the other hand, to be able to answer it is to be aware of much that has to do with Christian education.

The basic statement is found in I Corinthians 10:31: "Well, whether

22

you eat or drink or whatever you do, do everything for God's glory." The fundamental Greek term for glory is *doxa* ("reputation"). It corresponds closely to the Hebrew word *kabod,* which means "to be heavy." Something glorious is illustrious or has an illustrious reputation because of its weight. As we say, "It carries weight." That this primary Hebrew significance was not to be lost in Greek translation seems clear from Paul's emphasis on it in the phrase, "an eternal weight of glory" (II Cor. 4:17). The New Testament follows the Septuagint in translating *kabod* with *doxa*.

How does weight or heaviness describe God? And, more to the point, what does it mean that we must do everything to make God heavy?

To speak of God as "glorious" means that He possesses an incomparable weight of greatness, majesty, splendor, honor. His possession of such qualities far outweighs the possessions of all others combined.

To glorify God, then, is not to *add* to His possessions, so as to make them heavier. Human beings cannot do that. And, after all, as the Creator and the Sustainer of the universe, He owns all things. Nothing can be added. He is infinitely glorious; He is perfect, and His glory cannot be perfected.

Rather, to glorify God is to *ascribe* to Him the full weight of all the qualities He already possesses. It is to ascribe to Him all (not one ounce less, so to speak) that He really is. And to "do everything (math included) for God's glory" is to do that thing in such a way that the full weight of God's relationship to it is acknowledged. To "glorify God," therefore, means to make God heavy in one's own sight or in the eyes of others, or both. When Christ commands, ". . . let your light shine in the presence of people so that they may see your fine deeds and glorify your Father who is in the heavens" (Matt. 5:16), He is ordering us to bring others to an understanding of God's transforming work in our lives so that they will ascribe to Him the full weight of honor and credit that is due Him for redeeming His people. When we do everything for God's glory, then, whatever we do, we do in such a way that God's splendor shines through; He is given all the credit.

To the humanist, God is a *lightweight:* He is of such little importance in education that He is not even mentioned. Man is given all the credit. The essence of humanism is that God has been weighed and found wanting. The world, and all that men do in it, is viewed entirely apart from God. Weight is given to man instead. Both in the ways in which study and research are carried on and in the ways in which results are interpreted and taught, no weight is given to God or His claims. His Word is ignored; indeed, in the public schools it is banned.

In contrast, Christian education must give full weight to God's part in creation and redemption. For the Christian teacher, God is a heavyweight. God's claims are weighty and given full weight in the manner in which research and study are conducted and in teaching; God is properly accorded His rightful place in all that is done and said.

Thus, in a sense, the Christianity of any education may be quantified. Again and again, at all points the basic question, in a dozen forms, may be asked: "What weight does God have in this?" And according to the response, one may evaluate any given system or element of education by the place and standing (weight) that it accords to God in its various aspects.

So, the glory of God in all things—including Christian education—is the believer's ultimate purpose. The final purpose of Christian education for a teacher, then, is to accord to God His rightful place in his preparation, in his instruction and in the example of his life. My contention is that this is the very flaw to be found in Christian education today: it is lightweight; God is not heavily enough represented in what is done.

But now we must ask, what are those more proximate goals and purposes that will enable Christian educators to accord full weight to God in their teaching? The entire book is an answer to that question, but especially those chapters that follow. Yet, here I shall mention those basic goals and purposes around which the rest cluster.

THE TWO COMMANDS

Biblically, what fundamental purposes does God set forth for education? That is to say, what purposes, when properly achieved, will accord Him the full weight of splendor that is due His Name? There are (at least) two, one of which has to do with creation, and the other, with redemption.

All of those who wish to forge a system of truly Christian education must come to grips with both the facts of creation and the facts of redemption. That they haven't done so accounts for much of the failure that we encounter in the field of education. The purposes of Christian education are to help students to understand and to relate to God, to man and to the rest of creation in terms of the biblical parameters of creation and redemption.

Two passages stand uppermost in consideration of these two important areas. They tell us about God creating and God redeeming. They are Genesis 1:28:

> God blessed them; God said to them: Be fruitful; multiply; fill the earth and subdue it; bear rule[1] over the fish of the sea; over the birds of the air and over every living, moving creature on earth (Berkeley),

and Matthew 11:28-30:

> Come to Me, all who labor and are heavily burdened, and I will refresh you. Put My yoke on you and learn from Me; I am meek and humble in heart, and you will discover refreshment for your souls. My yoke is easy to wear and My burden is light.

Let us now consider each passage.

Genesis 1:28 does not relate directly to education, but only indirectly. Nevertheless, it sets forth very vital information about the role of man and woman in the earth, a role that has everything to do with education. Human beings glorify God only when they properly fulfil God's role for them. And education plays a part—not the whole as some educators think—in enabling man to fulfil that role. Though education's part is but a part, it is a significant part.

THE CREATION COMMAND

First, let us consider God's words to Adam and Eve: "God blessed them" (that is to say, God did good to them by declaring what follows and by conferring on them the right and the power to do it;[2] to bless someone, literally, is to say something good to him). He granted them the blessings of fruitfulness and rule, each of which was given in the form of a responsible command. Thus, from the outset God taught man that he was blessed both with privileges and with responsibilities. (It would be interesting, but here would take us too far afield, to pursue the

---

1. See also v. 26. Here we see that their rule extends to all the creatures and to "all the earth." This phrase, in v. 26, seems to correspond to the phrase, "and subdue it [the earth]." The word "subdue" means to "tread on," "to bring under subjection." It is used elsewhere of the active process of bringing under one's control (cf. Num. 32:22, 29; Josh. 18:1; Judges 3:3ᶜ; 4:23, etc.). It does not mean merely to exercise control or to rule, even though that idea is included in it. While ideas of organization and administration are inherent in it, the focus is on the *conquering-and-controlling* of that which previously was not in one's power.

2. Cf. v. 22.

idea of responsibility as a blessing.) This dual emphasis cannot be separated as modern humanistic education (and much so-called Christian education, following its lead) has tried to do. There is a commanding side to education. Education is not optional. When this divine imperative is divorced from education, God is not glorified; education loses its proper motivation and man is given discretionary powers that do not belong to him.

The plural in the phrase, "God blessed *them* and said to *them* . . . ," indicates that "man" in verses 26 and 28 is used generically for "mankind." That fact also means, as Calvin says, "This authority was not given to Adam only, but to all his posterity as well as to him." Thus, today the same purposes persist. Those purposes are to occupy (fill) and to control (subdue) the earth. Two of the ends of education, then, are to foster human social and political institutions (including the family[3]) and to nurture sciences and other controlling activities, to the glory of God. That is to say, education is for the purpose of bringing about proper ways of world occupation and control of the earth, ways that accord God His rightful weight. That this purpose still persists is clear from Genesis 8:17, where the command to occupy is repeated to fallen man (see also 9:1, 7): "God blessed Noah and his sons and told them: Be fruitful, multiply and populate the earth. . . .As for you, be fruitful and multiply; swarm over the earth and multiply in it." (Berkeley). And in Psalm 8:6, speaking of man, the psalmist says, "You made him to have dominion over the works of Your hands." If this is a prime purpose of creation, then education must make it a prime purpose as well. Education must study the ways and the means for Christians to fulfil that purpose.

God determined to fill the earth with human beings from one pair rather than populating the entire earth at once; accordingly, He gave the occupying task (how to go about doing this) to man himself. Also, few of the earth's resources, which God provided, were immediately available to man; accordingly, God assigned him the subduing task, in which those resources would be uncovered and utilized. To occupy and subdue to God's glory was man's *role* in the world. All education, then, in one way or another, should further these two creation purposes.

---

3. Biblical sex education, therefore, is very much a part of *Christian* education. Contrary to the world, in Christian education it is taught in the moral-family context of the Bible.

All of the processes that are involved in the human relationships of family, society, politics, business, church, as well as every other conceivable aspect of interpersonal relations, are bound up in the command to occupy. The command to multiply and to fill the earth could not be carried out apart from involvement in all of these areas; Christian education, therefore, will be concerned with discovering and with disseminating those principles and practices of occupation that glorify God. Moreover, the very outworking of the command to occupy is itself educational in nature. That is to say, it requires man to devise ways of relating human beings to one another, and to the earth, according to biblical principles.

Though Conant failed to notice that fact, as it applies to the occupying task, he does give evidence of understanding this principle at work in the task of subduing:

> What an education for the race has been this labor of subduing the earth! How it has developed reflection, stimulated invention, and quickened the powers of combination, which would otherwise have lain dormant.[4]

It is clear that all proper scientific endeavors to bring the creation into man's control are just as surely educational in nature. The fact is, then, that God set before the human race a vast enterprise, a significant part of which involved man's education about the nature and the control of the world and the human race that was to occupy it.

The earth, and all in it—both the animate and the inanimate creation—was given to man to *rule*. The rule of man, as God's superintendent of His earthly creation, was to be exercised through occupying the whole of it (Acts 17:26) and by bringing all under his control (cf. the "all things" of Ps. 8:6).

So, to summarize, we may say that one major purpose of the education of a human being must be to teach him how to rule over the creation in ways that honor and please God. To teach him to do so will require education that deals with all aspects of human occupation of the earth (people-oriented studies) and about all aspects of bringing the earth under his control (animal- and thing-oriented studies). Human relations, in all their possible forms, and the care and use of animals and the

---

4. Thos. J. Conant, *The Book of Genesis* (New York: American Bible Union, 1868), p. 7.

physical universe, in relation to man, are consequently the territory of education.

THE FALL

But we must now consider the effects of the fall on man's rule. Clearly, in the fall, human relationships with God, with man, and with the creation suffered. Adam died spiritually the day he ate of the forbidden fruit. Thus he died in his relationship to God. Moreover, that day he also began to die physically. His relationship to his fellow human beings was perverted. And, instead of subduing the earth, it now became the rule for man to be subdued by it. It is ironical that the one who was created to subdue the earth is now buried in it. Man lost his ability to build families, businesses, and other social structures that are free from error, sin, trouble, heartaches and other problems. Occupation and control of the earth and its resources has continued, but in harmful ways. Not only does the earth fight back with thorns and weeds (and all that this signifies), but wars and conquest have characterized the spread of the human race around the globe. And in subduing the earth man has depleted it, misused it, and created problems of pollution. All of this— and much more—is the result of Adam's sin.

In the fall man lost his rightful place of dominion, and though, through some native urge, he struggles yet to realize a selfish, humanistic version of occupation and control, in the end—as the writer of Ecclesiastes so pointedly observed—all his efforts end in disappointment and frustration.

Why is that? Because in the fall man chose to believe the father of lies rather than the Father of lights. And in subjecting himself to sin and to Satan, the latter became the "ruler of this world" (John 12:31). Satan took man's rightful place from him. Only in Christ, who wrested the right to rule from him, can man once again enter into the true fulfillment of the creation command. Apart from Christ he now serves sin and reaps the fruit of his sin in the form of trouble, misery and sorrow, here and hereafter. As Ecclesiastes puts it, "all is vanity [emptiness]." Apart from Christ all is *worthless*. That is to say, in terms of what we have been studying, it lacks *weight*. When God's glory is removed from the tasks of life, they become worthless. They lack meaning, purpose and signifi- cance. The splendor and magnificence has gone: across all of life is written *Ichabod*, "the glory has departed."

In Ecclesiastes 1:12-18, the preacher says that even with all of the opportunities and pleasures that kingship and great wisdom provided, a search for worldly knowledge left him totally disillusioned and dissatisfied. He found no joy or contentment in it—only weariness and sorrow. His conclusion was,

> For with much wisdom comes much sorrow; the more knowledge, the more grief (1:18, NIV).

That is Solomon's opinion of non-Christian education.

Adler taught that each man needs significance. In a distorted way, he came close to a truth: there must be significance to life to make it worth living. But Adler thought that each person was capable of finding significance in himself. He wrote these totally humanistic words:

> Every human being strives for significance; but people always make mistakes if they do not see that their whole significance must consist in their contribution to the lives of others.[5]

Such humanistic altruism will not satisfy. Sinful human beings are *not* significant, even when they "contribute." Solomon wrote, "I have seen all the works that are done under the sun; and, behold, all is vanity and chasing after the wind."[6] Significance cannot be found in man; that is one of the great messages of the Book of Ecclesiastes. And that is one reason why all education that leaves God out is sheer folly. Life has meaning and significance only in relationship to God. Sooner or later, those who follow Solomon's course also discover for themselves that there is no "weight" in intellectual pursuits—indeed, that they have been chasing the wind in all such activities—unless these pursuits are done for God's glory.

This means that, apart from Christ, even education that purports to provide one with what is needed to occupy and control the earth is vanity. Surely, in the course of human history, some principles of business and social life have been discovered and may be communicated to others; certainly, many scientific facts have been learned and may be taught, but the whole enterprise of teaching these, mingled as they are with falsehood, distortions and misapplications, and used as they are for selfish, man-centered ends, at length also reveals the poverty of pagan education. Such pursuits leave one with a humanism and scientism that

---

5. Alfred Adler, *What Life Should Mean to You* (London: Unwin Books, 1962), p. 13.
6. Or "vexation of spirit" (Eccles. 1:14).

ultimately call for the worship of man rather than God. And yet, it is men, like one's self, with whom one has all of his problems. Men kill, rape, steal, lie, slander; how, then, can there be any significance in serving man? Comte's positivism, with its worship of man, did not get very far. It was too open, too much out front. Man will not usually worship man knowingly; the worship of man must be disguised as humanitarianism, altruism, etc.

So, we must conclude that, since the fall, the creation command to rule by occupation-and-control-of-the-earth is, in itself, insufficient for sinful man. Likewise it is an insufficient educational goal. Unwittingly, however, pagan educators seek to fulfil their own dim visions of it, but whenever they think long and hard about what they are doing, they must say with Ecclesiastes, "It's all really worthless."

It is not the creation command that is vain; man himself is empty. It is he who lives a meaningless life and who brings his emptiness to the command, and to all else that he attempts in life.[7]

Man creates his own problems, and finds himself chasing after the wind (a hopeless and frustrating task) when he chases after meaning and significance in himself or in others like himself. It is only when one seeks first the kingdom of God and His righteousness that he finds meaning and begins to fulfil the creation command in any meaningful way. The creation command is good and righteous; and it still holds today. But sinful man cannot fulfil it. And one of the most frustrating aspects of all is that in the vain pursuit that he carries on he comes to realize that there is something always illusive and never really attainable, something just beyond his reach, that he senses could pull it all together for him. What he fails to realize is that the "something" that he seeks is really *Somebody:* the glorious, majestic, splendid God of creation who alone can give purpose, meaning and unity to life and to education.

THE REDEMPTIVE COMMAND

Because the creation command is weak through human sinfulness,

---

7. It is not that unsaved man recognizes the existence of God's command, but it seems that the impetus of occupying and controlling activities, by some innate urge within man himself, pushes all men to strive for civilization, culture and scientific dominance of some sort in the earth. But just as do-it-yourself legalism that attempts to save one from sin and its consequences fails, so too, this unaided attempt to achieve occupancy and control of the earth is doomed.

and among unredeemed sinners can never provide the satisfaction of serving God for which it was designed, there must be added to it a redemptive command as well. That command was issued by the Redeemer Himself, who said, "Come to Me, all who labor and are heavily burdened, and I will refresh you" (Matt. 11:28). It sounds almost as if He were responding directly to the writer of Ecclesiastes who, setting forth the unregenerate view of life, said, "I devoted my life to study and to explore by wisdom all that is done under heaven. What a heavy burden God has laid on men!" (Eccles. 1:13). Typically, the pagan blames God for the burden that man bears. But the burden is actually of his own making: he can rightly blame no one but himself. It is a burden he bears because of sin. And that he continues to labor under such a burden in spite of the Savior's gracious invitation to lay it down and receive refreshment, only emphasizes the fact.

What is this invitation? It is an invitation to lay down the burden of meaninglessness and frustration once and for all. It is an invitation to drink instead of the refreshing waters of satisfaction and purpose, which are to be found in Jesus Christ alone. Indeed, it is more than an invitation; it is a precious command. The Greek word *deuro,* with which this exhortation is introduced, is an *active* invitation usually accompanied by a gesture of the hand beckoning and urging another to come over where one is. "Here, over here," says the Lord; "here is the place to come," says Christ as He motions to sinful, frustrated men.

What is this invitational command to lay down sin's burden and find salvation's refreshment? It is an *educational* invitation; it is an invitation to *discipleship.* Christian education—truly *Christian* education—is the cause that refreshes!

Through His saving and sanctifying truth Christ promises to "refresh." The word in the original is a verb, as I have translated it in *The New Testament in Everyday English* ("I will refresh you"), and not a noun ("I will give you rest") as the King James Version weakly translates it. Christ, Himself, refreshes the weary, worn sinner who turns to Him.

This call to discipleship (a disciple = a pupil, a student) I said is in educational terms. How do I know that?

In verse 29, Jesus commands, "Put My yoke on you and learn from Me." That sentence is an invitational command to become His disciple.

To "put on the yoke" was an educational phrase well known to the Jews. In Lamentations 3:27, Jeremiah wrote that it is "good for a man to bear the yoke when he is young." And in Sirach 51:25 we read, "Put your neck under the yoke and receive instruction." To "bear the yoke" or "put on the yoke" meant, as Jesus explained, to "learn" from Him by becoming His student.

The Pharisees, in contrast, had placed heavy burdens on their disciples' backs that they could not bear. They taught that men must find meaning and purpose in themselves by keeping the law and their traditions, by which they thought they could be saved. Yet they did nothing to relieve them of these burdens (their legalistic, humanistic system was impotent; it could relieve no one of sin or of its consequences). On this point Matthew 23:4 and Acts 15:10 are explicit:

> They tie together heavy loads and put them on people's shoulders, but they don't want to lift a finger to budge them (Matt. 23:4).

> Now then, why are you testing God by putting on the disciples' neck a yoke that neither our fathers nor we have been able to bear? (Acts 15:10).

But, in this invitation, there is more than the relief that comes from laying down a load too great to carry; it is an invitation to refreshment. Salvation not only lifts the crushing burden; it also means the beginning of a new relationship to God and a new life to be lived for His glory. Forgiveness by faith brings an end to the old life while it introduces us to a new one. No man can happily be without a burden—tasks to perform in life. To those weary of laboring under a crushing load, Christ offers education for tasks that can be a joy.

Jesus is speaking to those who are weary of trying to live a life devoid of direction and power, to those whose study and understanding of life have turned to frustration and drudgery. He is addressing those who see life divided into so many unrelated, meaningless disciplines or duties that have neither unity nor any principle by which they may be integrated. To all such persons He calls, saying, "Let Me relieve you of your burden of sin with all of its effects." But, at the same time, He also calls them to a life of purpose and direction, which will honor God and be a pleasure and a delight to them. It is a way of life in which the creation command can come alive again. To all such He says, "Put on My yoke [i.e., become My disciple] and learn from [study with] Me."

Note, those who leave their burdens are not idle; they must take up new ones. The old ways of life that led to frustration and sin are exchanged for new ones. They are to "learn from" Christ, or, as those words might be translated, "be discipled by" Him. That means that not only will they learn *about* salvation (one cannot be a disciple apart from saving faith in Christ's death and resurrection), but, having been saved, they will go on to learn all that this salvation is *about*.

Christ's call is to come to Him, laying aside the burdens of sin. These burdens are found in:

1. *Humanism:* you must do it all on your own;
2. *Relativism:* nothing is ever certain or true, and there are no limits or absolutes;
3. *Experientialism:* you will have to find out for yourself, usually, the hard way—but you will never *really* find out at all ("ever learning and never coming to a knowledge of truth");
4. *Meaninglessness:* you can hang facts out to dry, flapping in the breeze, but (to change the figure) you won't be able to find a skewer with which to integrate them;
5. *Futility:* like the writer of Ecclesiastes, you'll find nothing but emptiness at the end of it all;
6. *Fear:* you'll spend your life in fear of the unknown and the known threats of life and of death, which will enslave you all of your days.

Christ delivers *from* all of these, and more—*to* their opposites. In Him, theism replaces humanism, absolutes replace relatives, revelation replaces experientialism, purpose replaces futility, faith and joy replace fear, and, in the end, heaven replaces hell.

That is the sort of educational enterprise to which Jesus Christ calls us. It is not rest—a mere relief from burdens—but it is refreshment, a rejuvenation of spirit that transforms a worthless, empty, meaningless existence into something glorious, something that has weight! It is education for a new life.

Until Christian educators see that this is what the original creation command itself involved—the joys and satisfactions of glorifying God in the earth that He created for doing so—that this is what man lost in sin, and that this is what must be restored in truly Christian education, we shall continue to limp along miserably, imitating and monkeying around with principles, practices, procedures, and processes that the world has devised—and is ever devising—in a hopeless attempt to find a way of interpreting life and educating for life. But, as Ecclesiastes makes clear, all such attempts are vain.

Christian education is a part of the work of Christ in enabling us to form a new, refreshing grasp on all of life so that we can live in new ways. It was intended, in all of its manifestations (in the home, the day school, the church, the college, the seminary) to be the cause that refreshes. Christ calls us to refreshment; and it is when we "learn from Him," rather than from the world, that we experience inner refreshment. If there is one thing that this careworn world needs, it is refreshment.

Unfortunately, however, we find children from our Christian homes heavily burdened down with their school work and school problems, just like children from pagan homes, who attend pagan schools. And this is not always because of their own negligence and other sinful propensities, though these are significant factors with which truly Christian education will deal. As a part of the learning experience to which Christ called us, Christian schooling itself must never add heavy burdens to students. Rather, it should delight. It ought to be plain to all that there is something radically wrong with Christian education when substantial numbers of children endure or even hate Christian school.

Christ's yoke—there is a discipline to His discipleship—is *"easy* to wear,"* and His burden *"is *light."* Christ puts us into harness, it is true, but the truth that He teaches (the yoke) is not a "yoke of slavery" (I Tim. 6:1); His truth, to which we submit, makes us "free." And the implications for accomplishing the tasks of daily living that we draw from this truth (the "burden" that we pull) do not tire us. This truth, instead, enables us to walk and run—and fly! (Isa. 40:31). John put it well when he wrote: "His commandments aren't annoying" (I John 5:3).

Christian schooling should not *add* to a student's burdensome life problems, as so often it does, wearing him out, discouraging, dispiriting and defeating him; rather, it should be a time of refreshment and rejuvenation that strengthens, encourages, inspires and enables him to live joyously amidst the other trials of life that he cannot avoid in a sinful world. It should be a relief from the chafing, galling burdens that a sinful society, by its false teachings and evil ways, tries to lay on him. It should be a preventive force in his life to help him avoid many of the crushing

34

burdens into which others, who know nothing of Christ's school of life, inevitably stumble.

What am I talking about? How does all this apply to a Christian teacher? Let me ask you: what is your work, anyway? What are you attempting to do? What is the redemptive goal of Christian education?

You must come to see yourself as a refresher, a rejuvenator of youth. That seems strange, I am sure. Even the words "refresher" and "rejuvenator" sound strange. But why? Because we have no specialized, accepted, technical term by which to express this concept. And that, unfortunately, is because we are totally unfamiliar with the concept of the teacher as refresher. When we have no word for a thing, an activity, or a concept, we do not recognize it in the cultures in which the word-deficient language is spoken. No wonder, then, that in Christian education it is necessary to go back to the blackboard and do our sums again.

As a teacher, administrator or parent, you must become thoroughly familiar with the concept and activity of refreshing, together with its implications, if you wish to get on with the business of educating in a truly Christian manner.

The Pharisees placed unbearable burdens on the backs of their disciples, and wouldn't help them to carry the load. In contrast, Jesus wants us to see to it that our precious children are put under His "easy" yoke to pull His "light" burden. It is a serious wrong for a teacher or parent to misrepresent Christ to his children by doing the opposite, in imitation of the world—especially when he does so in Jesus' Name. If education isn't freeing and refreshing, then it isn't Christian.

Teacher, ask yourself, "Are my students often excited and thrilled about their school work?" Ask, "Am I?" And further, "Do they and do I end the day, though physically tired, refreshed in spirit more often than not?" If they don't, something is wrong. That should be the rule for teachers and students at a Christian school. That is the sort of school that Christ is running; are you a part of it?

Parent, ask yourself, "Do my children frequently come home from school tired, but nonetheless happy, running over with the day's activities and learning, or is there a disproportionate number of days on which they come home drained, discouraged, dour or even apathetic about school?" If the latter is your common experience, something is wrong and must be corrected; school should be a soul-refreshing experience for them.

Well, perhaps you are thinking, "Does this mean that we must eliminate all the hard work at school? Does it mean that we must take seriously the etymology of the word "school" (from the Greek, *schole,* which means "leisure"), and turn the school into a country club?"

No, in the sort of educational program that I shall describe in this book, students will be motivated to work harder and longer than at present, simply *because* what they are doing is refreshing. Christ is speaking of the rest and refreshment of the soul, not of the brain or the rest of the body. The right sort of work, pursued in the right way, properly assigned by the right sort of person, for the right sort of reasons, can be quite refreshing, even when hard and exhausting.

For years I counseled 10 hours a day, twice a week. Often, when I began I was tired, sometimes even feverish. Yet, almost always I went home refreshed at the end of the day, and when there was fever, it was shaken. Remember Christ's words in John 4:31-34, when He spoke of "food" that the disciples knew nothing about. His food—that which strengthened, refreshed and revived Him in the midst of labor—was doing God's will (see v. 34). Hard work in school is like that when it is done under Christ's yoke, pulling His burdens. There is a refreshment of achievement in glorifying God with which nothing else can be compared. Of course, in a world of sin, with imperfect teachers and students, it will not always be so. But to the extent that we follow Him, Christ relieves us of Adam's curse of sweat by refreshing us.

The teacher's task, then, is to teach in such a way that his students become Christ's students and achieve what Christ expects of them. By pleasing Him, as a by-product, they will "discover refreshment" (Matt. 11:29c).

As we see from Christ's words about the Pharisees, and from much of what is called Christian education today, there is teaching, and a way of teaching, that is oppressive, crushing. It adds to Adam's curse. Such teaching is not Christ's teaching; His yoke never galls. It is "easy to wear."

But there *is* a yoke to wear; Christ puts His students into harness. There is much to be taught and much to learn. So too, the Christian teacher must yoke his students to himself under Christ. The "yoke" speaks of the authoritative parent-child relationship of the teacher and his disciple. The student submits to the teacher to learn and to do what he is taught. But I shall have more to say about discipleship in another place. Here I want only to observe this: precisely because teaching is yoking, we must be all the more careful to see that the yoke is easy to wear. Galled necks on Christian students are an infallible sign of faulty teaching, either in its methods, content, relational aspects, or all of these together.

In conclusion, I must add a word to the teacher from this passage. Let me ask you, "What kind of person are you? What is it like to study with *you?*"

The Pharisees were professionals who really didn't care all that much about their disciples, as we have seen. They arrogantly heaped burdens on others, but wouldn't lift a finger to help carry them. Some teachers in our Christian schools come close to that. "I gave it to them; they can take it or leave it," "the student is the enemy" (spoken in jest, but often not altogether so), and "teaching would be great if it weren't for the students," are sentiments that express the attitude of such persons. Too often you can find the professional academe in the Christian school, even without looking very hard; he is there because he is a professional. His interests are in *himself as a teacher,* not in the student. Teacher, are you like that? That sort of thing often develops in time when the teacher becomes disillusioned, and finds that what he is doing does not refresh either himself or his students. That's when he turns professional.

But listen to Christ, in this rare disclosure, as He describes His attitude toward teaching, and the kind of teacher that we find Him to be: "I am meek and humble in heart." Clearly, there is no professionalism in that. Does that strike you as the typical sort of teacher that you meet in a Christian school? It should. Fortunately, there are a large number of teachers who are humble, who have not yet been destroyed by the system.

But, if you are His disciple, you will become like Him (Luke 6:40), and that means not only as a person but as a teacher. If that is so, then it is important to understand what He means by these two descriptions of Himself.

Christ was "meek." Meekness is not weakness. It is a kindness and gentleness that grows out of concern. Christ cares for the student and, therefore, is caring to him. He is definitely *not* forbidding, unapproachable, formidable as some teachers are (and even pride themselves on being). Perhaps the best description of this quality is found in the way that James describes God the Father as teacher:

> So if any of you lacks wisdom, let him ask God for it, since He gives to everyone unreservedly and without reproaching, and it will be given to him (James 1:5).

With some teachers to approach is to broach reproach! That was never true of Christ; to the sincere learner, He always was easy to approach.

Christ also was "lowly [humble] in heart." This lowliness was "in *heart.*" That means that His lowliness was genuine. He did not merely appear to be lowly; He really was. "In heart" here means in His innermost being. Inwardly, Jesus was exactly what He appeared to be outwardly. His lowliness was a part of His essential make-up as a person; He was lowly through and through.

But what is lowliness? It is the opposite of all that characterized the scribes and the Pharisees as teachers. There was no pride or arrogance expressed in His content, or in His manner of presenting it. There was no professionalism that came between Him and His students.[8] Unlike some teachers, He never gave any student or group of students a hard time unnecessarily. He made learning itself a delight, a pleasure, easy—although the directions that He gave His students were not always so easy to follow in life.

In conclusion, it is important to realize that it is only the right purposes that can lead to the acquisition and development of the right personnel, doing the right sorts of things in the right ways in Christian education. The spin-offs from these two goals—the creation goal and the redemption goal—are numerous. Throughout the remainder of the book we shall be looking at many of them. But it is here, with an understanding of the purposes of Christian education, that we must begin. Otherwise, all else will go astray.

Education has, as its function, the task of introducing people to Christ's liberating, refreshing teaching about life in all its perspectives,

---

8. Jesus struck hard at professionalism when He said, "call nobody father," "do not let the people call you rabbi" and "do not let people call you leaders" (Matt. 23:8-10). Here He condemns the love of rank, titles and distinction that many teachers find so attractive. Such a yearning for titles in a teacher is the clearest evidence of his lack of satisfaction in the work that he is doing; in order to find some reward, he focuses on the accouterments of teaching (titles, honor, degrees) rather than on the joys of teaching itself.

which will enable them to enter into the occupying and controlling activities that were the substance of the creation commandment. This redemptive work of Christ in believers enables them to give God His full weight in all these endeavors.

7

THE FINAL PRODUCT

To sum up what we have learned in the previous chapter in a somewhat different way, we may say that the general purpose of Christian education is to help a student to become more like Christ. That means that Christian education must help him to leave behind those vague and vain views of living that, before conversion, kept him from glorifying God in his pursuit of life. It also means that he will be discipled into participation in the occupying and controlling activities to which God has summoned him. It must free him from those unbelievable burdens to which sin had yoked him and that caused him so much grief and misery. This happens only to those who trust Christ as Savior and begin to occupy and control in whatever ways they are able by the wisdom of God in the Scriptures and by the gifts and power of the Spirit. Thus, his education makes it possible for him to become more and more like Christ.

These purposes were considered in the form of basic, long term goals. Similarly, the summary statement in the first paragraph of this chapter is painted in broad strokes of the brush. But, if a graduate is to look like Christ, it is time to set forth some of the specific characteristics of Jesus as a person, which Christian education may rightfully endeavor to foster in the lives of students.

Here I shall list some of these characteristics together with some detail about what each involves, but I cannot now discuss how these characteristics may best be developed, or even treat each in depth. Educational ways and means must be considered later on, and many details about curriculum (for instance) must await further work by those who actually participate in the program in the days to come. The lists that follow are not exhaustive, but they afford the educator a starting point. Doubtless, he will wish to add to it. In chapter 19, item 1, you will find more material that might have been added here.

Jesus' mission focused on persons. He came to seek and to save those who were lost. Occupying concerns loom large, therefore. He died for

His *people,* not for inanimate objects or for the animal world (though His death has impact on both), so we should not expect to see Him engaged in controlling activities, or speaking about them so fully as occupying and redemptive concerns. Of course, all proper controlling involves occupying, and all proper occupying involves controlling; society and the non-human environment cannot be separated. Each affects the other. And, to add another dimension, since the fall, both must be carried on redemptively in order to please God.

That Jesus was not oblivious to the controlling task is clear from His miraculous and powerful control over the creation. As He healed diseases by supernatural means, in a lesser way men now do so by means of medicine. So too, we may seek to develop, by natural means, many of the controls over nature that he exercised in a miraculous way. Even in this way if we have eyes to see and ears to hear, it may be that He will provide leadership for our controlling activities. But that is largely conjecture, and I shall not spend time with it.

Among the occupying concerns to which Jesus addressed Himself are interpersonal relationships that have to do with God, the church, the world, the devil, the state, culture, one's neighbor, business, the home, and individuals in general. What Jesus had to say about each, and how He related to each, is a subject larger than I could even begin to explore here. Indeed, the matter would provide material for several books (which, by the way, ought to be written).

To fill the earth (the occupying task) demands comprehensive biblical consideration of at least each of these social areas of interpersonal relations. No one's education is complete without such considerations. And yet, some of the areas on the list are totally avoided not only in humanistic education, but in Christian education as well. But if, as the final product of Christian education, one is to become a person who shares the same values, beliefs, commitments and stances toward each occupying area that Jesus did, His concerns also must be a part of Christian education.

Among the controlling factors to which Jesus alluded is the question of unclean animals as food (Mark 7:19), His great use of nature for illustrations of spiritual truth, the healing of disease, His power over demons, etc. His miracles, in a very special way, demonstrate control over the world that is far superior to anything that science is able to achieve. However, much of what He did, as I suggested, might point to goals that science may—in its own non-miraculous realm—seek to approximate.

The occupying and controlling activities of Christ were not solely responses to the creation commandment (to occupy and to control); they were intermingled with His redemptive activities as well. In other words, we see in Jesus, and in His manner of approaching society, for instance, a condemnation of sinful hypocritical practices (corban, the sabbath traditions of the elders, ritualism, etc.) and the establishment of new principles of godly living. He gave us many of these principles both negatively and positively in the Sermon on the Mount and then, by His Holy Spirit, amplified and demonstrated them in the writings of His apostles, who applied them to specific life situations. His views of society, then, were not neutral. He mixed values with every statement about society. He called for action and belief in relationship to it, and indeed, related it all to Himself. Christian education must do the same.

As the Redeemer, all that He did and said was redemptive. He lived life as it ought to be lived, setting the standard for redemptive living today. And by His death, ascension and power He sent the Holy Spirit (to give new life, and ability to live it abundantly) to those that He regenerated, enabling them to walk "in His steps" as He commanded.

What Jesus taught us, by precept and by example, was that all of life had to be redeemed in order to fulfil the creation commandment. He made it clear, both by His confrontations with the religious leaders of His day and through the writings of the apostles, that apart from regeneration it is impossible to please God in anything. A Christian now fulfils the creation command redemptively.

Christ's example, standing in stark contrast to much in our lives, powerfully reinforces these facts. Therefore, as we contrast our own failures with His successes, we become painfully aware of the need to accept His redemptive offer. The priorities of man since the fall have changed. Creation commands (including the Ten Commandments, which are largely, though not exclusively, occupying commands) no longer come first in order of fulfillment. It is impossible to obey these commands, except merely outwardly (which is unacceptable), if one starts with creation rather than with redemption. The creation command must be understood, applied, and carried out redemptively.

That means that all other study, apart from the study of the way of life, is futile. And it means that pursuit of the creation command by itself can

42

be positively harmful as it was in the case of the Pharisees who refused to trust Christ because they saw no need for Him (cf. John 9:40, 41). They were wall-to-wall humanists, as indeed all are who follow the creation command apart from the redemptive command.

The whole ministry of Christ, then, both by precept and by example, puts emphasis on the necessity and the priority of the redemptive command, not only for salvation, but also in order to obey God in any occupying or controlling task. Danger to one's self (the self-deception of hypocrisy and its temporal and eternal consequences) and to others (the uses to which power over the universe is put by unregenerate persons— cf. some current proposals concerning the genetic control of life) can only be the outcome of placing priority on creation tasks while avoiding, delaying or excluding concern for the redemptive command of Christ.

All of this teaches us that if a person is truly regenerate and sanctification is occurring (i.e., he is being set apart more and more from sin to God), the proper conditions, including right attitudes, concerns, values, etc., for fulfilling the creation command, then—and only then—will prevail.

What sorts of attitudes do we see in Christ that are necessary for properly pursuing the creation task? These will be the proper attitudes for pursuing education. The two go together.

Rather than arbitrarily constructing a set of categories, let us consider the life and example of Jesus under the rubrics of that list of qualities known as the Spirit's fruit: love, joy, peace, patience, kindness, goodness, faithfulness, meekness and self-control. While the list itself is not complete, it is important and suggestive enough to give us a start in what we are concerned to do.

EDUCATION IS MORAL

But before entering into this study, let me emphasize an essential biblical principle that has been lost sight of in education and that underlies the analysis that I am about to make: *education is a moral activity.* Education is a behavioral, not merely an intellectual, affair. That this is so will be shown later on in depth, but for now note that this is taught explicitly in the Bible. Here are a few examples of such teaching:

1. *Doubt* is a matter that figures prominently in learning. It is of significance to educators, therefore, to know that James considers it a moral issue (see James 1:5-8; 4:8-10). To clear away doubt, James

makes plain, repentance is necessary.

2. In I Corinthians 1, 2, Paul compares and contrasts the *wisdom* of men with the wisdom of God and indicates that one's entire outlook on life is affected adversely apart from regeneration and the possession of the enabling Spirit. He divided all human beings into natural and spiritual persons. In I Corinthians 2:9 Paul says that it is not possible for the natural person (the one without the Spirit) to see, hear, understand or believe those things that God has prepared for spiritual persons (those with the Spirit). The former are so impoverished by their lack, according to I Corinthians 2:14-16, that they

(a) are unable to accept the Spirit's viewpoint on life (v. 14), a detriment that throws all education askew,

(b) cannot understand the Spirit's words (v. 13), which means that a biblical education is unavailable to them,

(c) cannot even understand the difference so as to discern what a spiritual person is.

In contrast, the spiritual person has been given all of these abilities. It is evident that all of them relate directly to one's understanding of and relationship to the world and life in it. God's world-and-life view depends on regeneration.

But does this spiritual impoverishment that is an outstanding characteristic of the natural person make a practical difference in how he lives? It certainly does:

> No modern day leaders have known this [God's wisdom]; if they had known they wouldn't have crucified the Lord of Glory (I Cor. 2:8).

Spiritual ignorance led to the greatest error and tragedy (though God planned and providentially used it as a divine success) in human history. If, as Paul teaches, spiritual impoverishment led to the ultimate and most basic crime of all—the crucifixion—is there any other act of villainy of which it is incapable? No, this is not merely some theoretical difference; it has very practical consequences.

3. Whole nations have been destroyed and civilizations wiped out and stricken with disaster, because of spiritual ignorance (cf. Jer. 8:9, 10; 9:17-24; Rom. 10:3). Hosea once lamented, "My people are destroyed for lack of knowledge" (Hos. 4:6).

4. Rejection of divine truth leads to immorality (cf. Rom. 1:21-32; II Pet. 2:1, 2; Jude 8).

5. Without the Spirit of God, no person can please God (Rom. 8:8).

The simple fact is that the Bible says that the learning that God approves is dependent on obedience (John 7:17). It is just as true that one must obey in order to know as it is that one must know in order to obey. That is the biblical view of education. The two are inextricably intertwined.

The Greek, academic idea of cognitive learning, which Western education has followed, emphasizes "facts" in isolation. In contrast, the biblical discipleship model is a moral model (I shall say more about discipleship later). In the Bible it is not only true that seeing is believing, but it is just as true that believing is seeing (John 10:38; 20:29). To know the truth, biblically speaking, is to "walk in the truth." Truth is learned and understood only as it is accepted fully by becoming incarnate in the learner. It must be perceived intellectually, then lived to be fully known. One must will to *do* God's will (John 7:17); it is not enough to will to *know* it.

If we want to turn out a final product that looks like Jesus Christ, we may no longer neglect the moral/behavioral side of education. That is why we must take another look at the fruit of the Spirit in the life of Christ. The Spirit's fruit is an educational matter.

THE SPIRIT'S FRUIT

Notice first of all that none of the nine qualities mentioned in Galatians 5 is purely cognitive. That is important. As I have been saying, each involves cognitive elements *integrated into character*. They are all facets of redeemed (or, in Christ's case, sinless) personality. That should tell us a lot about the finished product of a truly biblical educational model.

Let us look, then, at the personality of Jesus through this 9-faceted grid. Because I have already studied the Spirit's fruit from other perspectives in *More than Redemption* (chapter 15), I shall try to repeat as little of what I said there as possible. Let me briefly define each word, then relate it to Jesus Christ.

Love

In the New Testament, *agape* (love) always is an outgoing element that is more than the benevolent feeling that accompanies it. Essentially, it is the determination to give of one's self to another. What man in all of history more untiringly or more freely gave himself to and for others than did Christ?

The very focus of His ministry was love undeserved and unreserved. And, His love, in all of life's relationships, is the pattern for ours (John 13:34a). The final product of any truly Christian education, when it takes hold, will be an outward-moving, giving person who in occupying tasks will give evidence of God's values. As a person, as a decision maker, as a worker he will be concerned about and will manifest love. The love of Christ will control him as he engages in controlling projects. His being a loving person will make a demonstrable difference readily seen in how he executes every task.

Education devoid of all concern for love is one of the great tragedies of our time. But how can love be taught and fostered apart from the teaching of the cross?

Joy

Seldom is Christ thought of as joyful. The phrases in Isaiah 53:3, "a man of sorrows, and acquainted with grief," are often misinterpreted to mean that Jesus was sullen, grim, and dour because He carried the load of the world on His shoulders and could never afford to smile. That is hardly the biblical picture. That He suffered and knew the miseries of suffering all too well is what Isaiah is telling us. But listen, this time, to how the Berkeley version, which more closely approximates the original, describes Jesus in the same verse: "a man of sufferings and acquainted with sickness."

Jesus was a man of joy. That is the wonder of joy—it can coexist with suffering. Note how Hebrews intermixes the two: ". . . looking off to Jesus the Author and Completer of our faith, Who, for the joy that had been set before Him, endured the cross, despising the shame, and is seated at the right hand of God's throne" (Heb. 12:2). There was joy and pain and shame on the cross. And it was Jesus who said that He wanted His disciples to experience the fullness of joy that He Himself had: "I have spoken these things to you so that My joy may be in you and your joy may be full" (John 15:11). To impart His joy meant that He first experienced it and was the Source of all true joy.

What is this joy? It is a deep-seated attitude of confidence that grows out of dependence on God; it is knowing that He "works all things after the counsel of His own will" (Eph. 1:11), and that "all things work

46

together for good" to His children (Rom. 8:28). Joy is deeper than happiness, which shifts according to the happenings on which it depends.

The person who has been educated God's way, like Christ, will have a joyfully realistic outlook on life and a joyful attitude to sustain him when the going gets tough in this sinful world. Students will learn much from this attitude. To lay the foundation for such an attitude when teaching history, for instance, the teacher must not only hold correct, biblical *views* of history, but also must himself *possess* this joy. If he does not, his outlook on history will be less than biblical. And, his students will be taught a warped view of history.

Peace

Peace, Paul informs us, "passes all understanding" (Phil. 4:7), and so it would be presumptuous and absurd for me to attempt to describe or define it. The *shalom* of the Bible is more than the cessation or absence of hostilities. It has rich positive associations. It is a sense of serenity that comes to one who has the knowledge not only that God's universe is running smoothly under His sovereign control, but that in Christ, he himself stands in a satisfactory relationship to both.

Jesus, the Prince of Peace (Isa. 9:6), is both the possessor and dispenser of peace. He was never ruffled, never distraught. He exhibited a calm and assurance that was the product of unalloyed peace. A person educated biblically also should exhibit something of this unperturbed calm because, like Christ, he also will be fortified against life's storms by similar inner resources. A peaceful person carries out his occupying and controlling tasks differently than a troubled one. The *shalom* of God has a lot to do, for instance, with one's attitudes toward the pursuit of science, toward his relationships in business or in whatever area the graduate may find himself at work.

Patience

Christ was also a man of great patience. He was full of *makrothumia* ("long-temperedness"). With superb patience, He coolly faced insults, blasphemy, accusations and every other form of temptation to which others of us would have succumbed. He never lost His temper, was always able to measure His words and, indeed, set the pattern for us by doing good to those who despitefully used Him. No person can be considered properly educated without learning the capacity for such self-restraint in whatever he does.

Kindness

Kindness refers to a special kind of caring concern for others that is opposed to all harshness, cruelty or severity. In Christ's dealings with repentant sinners, the presence of this quality may often be discerned as a dominant note in the story. There is a tenderness about Christ—what He does, and how He does it—that has had a transforming effect on the values of the world; plainly, Christian education should strengthen this quality as well as infuse it into every activity.

Goodness

If kindness is a special kind of caring concern for others, goodness is the *demonstration* of that concern. Goodness is the outgoing *activity* of a kind spirit; it is its *expression* in concrete *deeds*. It is not enough to have a kind attitude if that attitude never leads to acts of kindness. Goodness refers to the efforts of a good, kind person to *do* good to others.

But doing good is doing what is good in God's sight. That is quite a different thing from the humanistic do-gooder ethics of liberal theology. Indeed, doing good, as God describes it, frequently will call forth acts opposite to those that are followed by humanists. Ultimately, whatever is good for the kingdom of God is good for the believer and for the world in general. Like Christ, a Christian must be educated to go about doing good in his occupying and controlling activities.

Faithfulness

Faithfulness is reliability, trustworthiness, dependability. Jesus, who is the ''same'' (you can depend on Him) ''yesterday, today and forever'' (Heb. 13:8), exemplifies that quality. Because He was faithful to God (Heb. 3:2), He is faithful to men. Education cannot be complete without the cultivation of this fruit in husbands/wives, employers/employees, etc. In no area of life can one be unfaithful and consider himself educated, in spite of the many facts that he may have accumulated. Faithfulness to man (as a researcher or a reporter who must faithfully use facts) begins with faithfulness to God.

Meekness

Probably this is the most misunderstood term of the lot. Many people equate meekness and weakness. Moses was meek but certainly not weak. Christ, as we saw in the previous chapter, called Himself meek. Meekness speaks of the gentle side of strength. The word embraces the idea of *soothing*. A meek person never creates or enlarges problems unnecessarily, never is loud, boisterous or boastful. His is the quiet strength of humility. In sore spots, a meek person knows how to soothe and heal. Education devoid of meekness is a buzz saw and a rasping file.

Self-control

Finally, this control over desire (not an autonomy of any sort) is necessary in every one of life's occupying and controlling activities. Until a person can say "not my will but Yours be done," as His Lord did, he is not ready to control any other aspect of God's creation. Controlling activities, for sinners, must begin with gaining control over one's self. The feeling-orientation of our society is directly opposed to self-control. Education can ill afford to proceed apart from self-control.

"But," you ask, "shouldn't a person learn these things in church?"

Yes, he should learn something of them there, but principally he will learn to effect what he has been taught on one day a week during the rest of the week as he puts biblical principles into practice in actual life situations. And, as you will learn subsequently, biblical education ought to be taught in the milieu. It should be kneaded into the dough of everyday tasks. When it is, it will be learned, because it will be learned for use, and the tasks themselves will be done differently.

WISDOM

Now, what have we discovered? Simply this: that "The fear of the Lord is the beginning of wisdom" (Prov. 1:7). The phrase, "the fear of the Lord," ought not to be translated, "reverence for the Lord," as some think. These words had become a technical phrase that, by the time Proverbs was written, meant *a godly lifestyle* (cf. Ps. 19:9; a godly lifestyle is a clean lifestyle). It is the Old Testament equivalent of John's "walking in the truth." It means living in the way that one who has awe and reverence occasioned by the knowledge of God's terror would live. As David indicated in Psalm 34:11, the fear of the Lord could be *taught*.

It is educational material. And in the verses that follow in the psalm, he describes the kind of life that *is* the fear of the Lord. Education, then, has a relational-moral side.

Wisdom cannot be divorced from character and behavior. Humanistic academes constantly attempt to do this. It is because this divorce is impossible that every attempt by Christians to clean up public education by eliminating pagan values is doomed to failure. The teachers in these schools would have to be converted and grow in grace for that to happen. It simply cannot be done otherwise. Wisdom, values and lifestyles are so integrally related to teaching that, whenever teaching is done, they are necessarily communicated. Either pagan wisdom or godly wisdom is communicated along with pagan or godly ways of life.

In I Corinthians 1 Paul says that there are two kinds of wisdom: worldly wisdom and God's wisdom. Unsaved teachers, who know nothing of the fear of the Lord, cannot teach God's wisdom. That is why only Christian teachers can teach in a manner that is acceptable to God. You might as well command cats to bark as to expect such teachers to stop teaching humanism—both its values and its ways of living. They *cannot* do so, even if they wanted to. All that such efforts ever accomplish is to exchange more obvious (and therefore more easily avoidable) forms of humanism for more subtle, and therefore, more dangerous ones.

No, the final product of a truly Christian education will be a person whose knowledge, skills, and lifestyle will all be set within the framework of the Spirit's fruit, which is only another way of saying that, like Christ, he will exhibit a life of love toward God and neighbor concretized by an experiential understanding of what keeping God's commandments means in relationship to the church, the world, the devil, the state, the culture, business, the home. All that he learns of facts, skills and ministries related to these occupying areas must be integrated with a lifestyle pleasing to God.

That I have spoken more of occupying activities than of controlling ones is natural because that is the focus of the Scriptures. But it is inevitable also because controlling activities like farming, science, and industrial enterprises can never be done in isolation. They affect people as individuals and as masses. And controlling activities must also be done *in relation* to God and neighbor. God has so ordered life that occupying activities depend on controlling activities and controlling activities depend on occupying activities. And both—to be done acceptably—depend on the fear of the Lord. Because you can't have either one without the other in God's world, you must not try to separate them in education.

EDUCATION FOR ALL GOD'S CHILDREN

A number of Christian day schools have become little more than prep schools that have as their goal a finished product acceptable for college. But this is an unworthy goal. There are at least two reasons why I can say that, realizing all the while that I am stepping on many toes:

1. *Every* Christian child should be educated for life. This is true whether he goes to college or not. Christian education for the elite can no more be justified than food, clothing or shelter for the elite. Indeed, education for life before God in His world is even more essential than those necessities. What is needed is an education that, while similarly training *all* in the fear of the Lord, at the same time distinguishes and separates according to gifts and sets each child on a course for his future, preparing him in whatever is necessary for excelling in what he should do. "But, we can't afford such diversified and individualized training," you may object. I disagree. Using the plan of education that I shall outline for you, it is altogether possible and entirely feasible to train each child differently, and it should cost you less. (In some cases, doing so may actually bring in financial returns to the school!) You are thinking of education as it is at present when you raise the objection. I will grant you that it would be too costly for that; doubtless, that is one reason why those who are considered non-college material are excluded or dropped by the wayside.

2. College preparation, as it is currently understood, is no more Christian than what is done in non-Christian schools. And, to boot, no one knows what constitutes "college preparation." Colleges differ so greatly in what they are looking for that there is no way of guessing beforehand what would be "good" preparation for any and all colleges. Ability to pass S.A.T. tests is, at the moment, the only sort of general standard available, and the program that I shall outline will more than prepare those who ought to go to college for that. But the S.A.T. is a hopelessly inadequate standard. Yet it is used by Christian colleges because they, like Christian day schools, also have been designed according to pagan models and have failed to develop Christian stan-

dards of admission. No less than grade schools, Christian colleges need a complete overhaul.[1] If anything, there is more vital Christian teaching in the better Christian day school—as deficient as that is—than there is in the average Christian college. After all, it is the Christian colleges, in the main, that are training the teachers for the grade schools. And it is those teachers who are crying, "Why didn't they tell me how to teach as a Christian should?"

No, the finished product of Christian grade schools should be a young man or woman who knows how to think and act biblically in all of life. He should be aware of his gifts and be headed toward a life specialty, on which he has already embarked to some extent while still in "grade" school. He should know how to distinguish God's wisdom from the wisdom of the world wherever he meets it: in advertisements, in books, in TV programs. He should know how to live as a Christian citizen under a government that doesn't always act Christianly. And he should be able to manifest the fruit of the Spirit in all that he does.

He should know how to use the Bible on Thursday,[2] at the office, on the farm, at home, and in whatever he is doing. He should know how to make God the interpretive thread that ties all learning together and puts meaning, value, purpose and goals into all of life. He must know all about God's world, his own body, and how to care for them. But, with all of his general knowledge, he must be already deeply involved in the area of life that he will probably enter when he is out of school. He should know this area in depth. "In depth" means not only a profundity of factual material, but a growing ability to plumb the depths of this area theologically. That, in turn, means that he must also know basic theology and how to use it in practical ways. A Christian knows that all of life

---

1. See Appendix A for a sketch of a suggested theological program. I have not developed a similar sketch of a college program, but, as a comparison of the theological program with the one I shall advocate for grade schools will reveal, the basic principles extend to teaching at all levels.

I have been considering the idea that college training may not be necessary. Perhaps, on leaving day school (parental education) a student ought to be trained by the state (if he will be involved in government), by the church (if his work will be ministerial), or by business (if he enters this area). Possibly day schools could be extended a year or two more if necessary. But I shall not discuss this matter here.

2. For more on this, see my book, *What to Do on Thursday* (Phillipsburg, N.J.: Presbyterian and Reformed, 1982). That book shows how to use the Bible practically when encountering problems in the course of daily life. It was designed for use with students in Christian day schools, in the church, or at home.

is interrelated because God made it. He expects to discover these interrelationships and possesses the integrating principle for doing so.

In short, his education must make it possible for him to have a specialty, and to be able to relate it to all of the occupying and controlling tasks of life that are connected to it. And he must be able to understand and integrate it into the whole of life in God's world. He must know how to function in relation to others in love, not only in the common situations of life, but particularly in the area of his specialty.

It is time that we stopped mimicking the schools down the street, setting goals that are fundamentally the same. When we unwittingly adopt goals that (if we thought about it) we don't believe in, they can do nothing for us but help produce a final product that we don't believe in either. That doesn't work; and it never will. Heated discussions on subjects like, "Should we teach facts or the process of thinking?" miss the point. Actually, they will not arise in truly Christian education as they do down the street, because, as you will presently see, when we follow biblical principles of teaching (such as learning for doing, discipleship teaching, and life-milieu teaching) problems like that are solved automatically. Biblical teaching does not divide facts from processes, or skills from knowledge because it teaches both at once in the same curriculum.

Pagan education is confused about the end product; that is why the graduates of pagan schools are confused. They are confused about life and their place in it, about what their responsibilities are, what they should (or can) do with what little they have learned, etc. It could not be otherwise for those who have spent 12 years in the dis-integrated, fractured, chaotic, changing and ill-conceived atmosphere that we call the public school. Why Christian school leaders wish to trail along, imitating this educational travesty, I have difficulty comprehending. Of course, historically, we see that Christian education, as we now know it, took the course of least difficulty: imitation with minimal modification. Now, in the midst of the present failure of Christian education to contribute any significantly different product, as painful as that realization may be, it is still easier to drift, justify, and complain. It appears that this is the simplest way to account for what has happened. After all, change, radical change of the sort that is needed, calls for risk, upheaval. Who wants to rock a boat that is laden down with cargo and far out to sea?

I do! And if you do too—in spite of the risk—read on. The way ahead is through posing and solving many problems God's way. That is what I propose to begin doing.

But in conclusion, let us see once more what the final product of Christian grade school education should look like. He should look as much like Christ as possible. Not that he can or even should do exactly what Christ did; clearly that isn't the goal. His calling and His ministry were unique. But in values, character, behavior, approach and life goals, in his specialty area, the graduate should think, speak and act as Jesus would.

8

THE RAW PRODUCT

Given the ideal of turning out a finished product that is as much like Christ as possible, we may ask, "How do we reach this ideal?" We may want to rephrase the question, "How do we even head in the direction that leads toward that ideal?"[1] Two answers may be given here:

1. We must discover what the raw product (A) is like.
2. We must develop ways and means (B) of moving students along from point A to C (the finished product).

Here is how it looks in diagram:

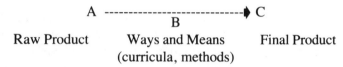

It is impossible to design B without first knowing all that it is necessary to know about C and A. Until we understand where we intend to go and where we are when we are about to begin travelling, we cannot plan the trip. Foolishly, many educators have been taking endless journeys from who-knows-where to who-knows-what. If you were to ask them, "What is it that you are trying to do?," they might be puzzled by the question and reply, "Well, I'm trying to educate these children, of course." But that meaningless response begs the question. The initial concern must not be how to educate, but *whom* to educate and for *what*. Both the biblical destination and the biblical starting point must be known if we wish to draw the straightest line between points A and C.

Of course, in one sense, all depends on where you are in the process. If you are teaching those of a certain age, who have (or should have) already been brought up to a certain level of proficiency by others, your *immediate* objectives might be different from those of the teacher who is about to prepare another group of students to send along to you, or from

---

1. Clearly, in a world of sin, even the best program will do no better than the sinners who participate in it.

those of the teacher who is about to begin working with the crop that you most recently passed on to him. (However, in the new education that I shall propose such grade levels will not mean as much.) But in this chapter those sorts of considerations are not in view. Here we shall consider the more fundamental question of the nature of the raw product with which teachers (at all levels) must work.

THE STUDENT

This person who must be taught has a duplex nature (for details on this, see my *More than Redemption,* pp. 110ff.). It is in part material and in part non-material; yet he must be dealt with as a whole person. In this life the two are inseparable. He is a moral being, created in God's image. He is now a fallen creature, who has (or has not) been regenerated, whose whole way of life is affected by sin and how he is handling it. All of this within one person demands a holistic approach to education. How foolish to try to educate only the mind, as academes do!

All of these factors will have a very great effect on how he learns. Moreover, he is an *individual* with *unique* gifts that must be discovered, developed and deployed for the glory of Jesus Christ and the welfare of his neighbor.

I am concerned, therefore, not only with the facts that he knows, and with the skills that he has learned, but how his relationship to God and to his neighbor affects education. Because Christians take seriously the fact that the Holy Spirit is involved in education, as Paul taught us in I Corinthians 2, not only is it tragic to by-pass such issues as those listed above, but it is impossible to do so and at the same time claim that the education that does is, at *bottom,* anything more than humanistic. These issues, then, will be our concern.

Whole books should be written on every one of the matters mentioned in the previous paragraphs. It would be unrealistic for me, therefore, to think that I could do more than raise a few issues, point in the direction of some answers to a number of questions, and attempt to suggest the solution to a few problems.

THE IMAGE OF GOD IN EDUCATION

The image of God in man is his high-level intellectual and moral capacity; it involves his ability to undertake the occupying and controlling tasks to which God called him. It enables him to sustain a moral, responsible relationship to God and to other men. In short, it involves his ability to comprehend, to accept, to live and to minister the truth; it is his basic capacity for occupying and for controlling tasks.

Of course, Christians know that the image was seriously marred by the fall. Man is still a moral, responsible creature, who now acts immorally and irresponsibly; he is still an intelligent being, who because of the fall acts irrationally and illogically. The capacity to sustain a relationship to God yet exists, but it is a relationship of enmity. Thus, the image of God in man—apart from regeneration—has been severely corrupted by the fall.

Every student has intellectual and moral capacity, but that has been affected by the fall. Either he is still a "natural" person, who is at enmity with God, or he is a regenerated person, in whom the Holy Spirit dwells and is at work restoring and refurbishing the image. That difference makes all the difference in the world.

The physical capacity for learning, though distorted, remains, even in unregenerate persons. That is to say, a human being is still a human being, even after the fall. That is why, in spite of the fall, the human race has snaked its way ahead, in misery, in the pursuit of occupying tasks (like government and politics) and in controlling tasks (like agriculture and dairy farming). I say "snaked ahead" in "misery" because of both the curse that God placed on the ground and the curse of the fall that is within man. These have greatly impeded progress, which has gone ahead by a very circuitous route, and allowed any forward movement only at great cost. The strained interpersonal relationships, human greed and avarice, the discouragements to which these lead, and the selfish pursuit of one's goals, plus his own lethargy and sinful propensities, are enough to turn the whole process inside out were it not for the common grace of God (the goodness of God given to all men alike), which (negatively) restrains human sin from going any further than it does and (positively) gives opportunity for some outward progress to all. But, apart from regeneration, there is no capacity for pleasing God. The human capacity that a natural person possesses is totally bent toward sin.

WHO IS EDUCABLE?

Of what consequence are these facts to Christian educators? They are of the utmost importance. Pagan educators know nothing of these facts about human nature and, therefore, fail to take them into account in their thinking and planning. Their systems make no provisions for dealing with sin and its consequences. They know nothing of two classes of men and two ways of learning, one purely human, the other aided by supernatural revelation and the power of the Holy Spirit. They assume (wrongly) that

(1) all persons with adequate mental ability are educable;

(2) all persons of similar mental ability are equally educable;

(3) all persons are educable by human means alone.

Every one of these far-reaching assumptions is false. Consider propositions 1 and 2. Are all persons educable? Yes, to a certain extent, in some things; but none is educable in God's wisdom, in God's worldview, or in ways that please Him apart from Christ. That means that in education that counts, only regenerate persons are educable. Pagan educators admit of no such distinction. But there is no equality, whatever, according to I Corinthians 2.

Consider also proposition 3. Educability is not a purely human activity. Prayer has a part in education (cf. Col. 1:9). God Himself is involved in teaching (cf. John 6:44, 45). Unregenerate persons are deprived of these influences. And, even a Christian will fail to learn facts as he ought to, will fail to integrate them into life, and will fail to make proper use of them in ministry as God requires him to, when he is disobedient to God his Father and unloving to others in the family of God. What then can be said of the unbeliever?

In other words, both one's judicial relationship to God and his familial relationship to Him will have great effect on the education that takes place at a particular time, or on any given day. The relationships of a believer at a given time in his life may have everything to do with learning. Neither pagan educators nor most Christian educators have come to grips with this all-important educational principle.

Opportunities for evangelism must be fitted into the educational system, as well as periods for confession of sin. Regular encouragement to be reconciled to others along with much individual counsel about every aspect of the student's relationship to God and his neighbor must be provided.

Moreover, schools must provide preventive instruction and exhortation, guidance around potholes in educational pathways and every other sort of positive help that is designed to lead students away from unnecessary temptations.

DIFFERING CAPACITIES

But if there is a fundamental distinction between the learning of regenerate and unregenerate persons, and if Christian education means becoming like Christ, then that raises any number of questions that must be answered. I am sure I do not have the answers to all of them, and a great amount of thought yet needs to be given to the matter.

The great problem that we face is this: it is impossible to educate unregenerate or rebellious Christian students Christianly. That such students will be a part of the educational program, whether we like it or not, is a fact. Perhaps in younger years, the majority of the students we teach, even those coming from Christian homes, will be uncoverted. How, then, do we handle this problem?

First of all, let us understand plainly that in this life we will never finally know who is regenerate and who is not. God has reserved the right of reading hearts for Himself: "Man looks on the outward appearance, but God looks on the heart" (I Sam. 16:7). Any judgments that are made—and the Christian school must make them—will be functional judgments, not final judgments. In judging functionally, you function toward one *as* a Christian or *"as* a heathen and a publican" (an unregenerate person). On this matter, study Matthew 18:17. The church may make this functional judgment whenever a professed member renounces Christ's authority by leaving the church (I John 2:19) or by continued refusal to submit to that authority under the discipline of the church (Matt. 18:17).

The same principle must be carried over into the Christian school. But there are some differences. Many children will enter school before they have made a public profession of faith in Christ, or before they have renounced Christ's authority. They will be uncertainties in the school just as they are in the home. This situation exists because, as I shall have occasion later on to show, the Christian school is an extension of the Christian home.

But if membership in the school depends on having at least one believing parent who is willing to pray for his child and to continue to introduce him to Jesus Christ (as it should), and if the school also continually makes an evangelistic effort, we may presume that at length

59

many—if not most—of the children in the school will come to know Christ as Savior at an early age. The "beginning of wisdom" often will take place as a part of the efforts of teachers who work with children of kindergarten and elementary age.

It is conceivable that many churches have waited too long to seek a public profession of faith. Should not children be confronted with the decision to trust Christ before or at the time they enter school? This should be done, of course, in proper ways, without any pressure. If one is old enough to begin formal education, is he not old enough to trust Him who is the Source of all wisdom and knowledge?

Every teacher in a school should conceive of himself as a parental evangelist. Because we do not ever know finally who is and who is not a Christian, it is important to keep the gospel before the student body at all ages throughout their entire time at school.

While there will be no judging of hearts, functional judgments will be made. It is necessary to do this in order to fulfil God's commands. Sometimes Matthew 7:1-5 is quoted to condemn all judgment. But that is precisely what it does not do. Just after warning against improper, unjust and blind judgment, Jesus commands:

> Don't give what is holy to dogs; and don't throw your pearls before pigs; otherwise they may trample them under their feet and turn on you and attack you (Matt. 7:6).

Clearly, this passage, which is so appropriate to Christian educators, counters the interpretation of Matthew 7:1-5 that understands the passage to prohibit *all* sorts of judgment, including proper functional judgments. In this very next verse, Jesus calls on us to judge between those to whom we shall give holy things and pearls and those from whom we must withhold them because they are "dogs" and "pigs" who are unfit to have them. What are these "holy things" and "pearls"? The two are unidentified in the passage, and just because these phrases are so indefinite, they are broad enough to encompass any and all Christian teaching and activities that should be directed to believers alone. We must judge who is and who is not a pig or dog to obey the command. The principle about pearls must guide the Christian school as well as any other appropriate body.

The school will patiently sow the seed, will discipline and nurture, will show individual concern for and make every effort to evangelize every student in both formal and informal ways. But, along the way, two factors will sort out those about whom a negative, functional (not final) judgment must be made:

1. *Unrepentant, contumacious immorality and/or insubordination* must be dealt with. This is a stubbornness and an ongoing unwillingness to submit to Christ's Word that should be grounds for dismissal from school. But, *first,* before dismissal, the matter ought to be pursued in the church to which the child belongs and under whose care and discipline he is. Full opportunity for repentance may not be determined to be complete until there has been full recourse to church discipline. And even after unsuccessful discipline and dismissal, the school, like the church, must be willing to restore a student if and when he returns in repentance. The school must work closely with the home and the church in such matters.

2. *Continued incapacity for understanding and application of Christian truth* is the second factor. This must not be a matter of an intellectual deficit, a question of misjudgment about gifts, and the like. Rather, it must be a total, across-the-board incapacity to grasp and use Christian principles. This must be so consistent and pervasive that it becomes apparent to all that the student's trouble is a problem with pearls.

What then? First, any such child should be confronted lovingly with the problem and his commitment to Christ (or lack of it) explored. Evangelism should be attempted (avoiding all improper pressure). His parents and church should be contacted and the problem should be explained to them. After failure by all parties concerned, the child will have to be dismissed. But this must not happen during his first few years at school. Remember, Jesus allowed Judas to remain in the school of the disciples for three and a half years!

In all of this we must not be hasty in the application of the principle about pearls. Yet, it must be remembered that because Jesus allowed Judas to remain and to walk on pearls, in the end Judas did "turn" and "attack" Him. Perhaps He wanted to spare us from what He willingly endured for our sakes. But, nevertheless, remembering Christ's patience with the other disciples—especially Peter and Thomas, who seemed not to believe until the very end—it is wise not to give up on any student too soon.

Will there have to be two tracks then—one for believers and one for those who are not? No. There was only one track among the disciples, even though each seemed to have received the gift of spiritual perception at a different time. There are not two tracks in the home (though adaptations often are made for seemingly unregenerate children and expectations differ). Much ignorance, due to moral problems, doubts, etc., later was replaced by faith, understanding and a change of life. Presumably, the experience and the teaching that the disciples had prior to that point was not in vain. Somehow, the Spirit of God was able to capitalize on it at the time of conversion and afterward (see John 2:22; Matt. 26:75; Luke 24:8; John 13:7). We do not understand this, but we believe it to be so. Similarly, in our homes, in obedience to God, from the earliest years, along with evangelism, we instruct and discipline our children in the ways of Christ (Eph. 6:4). Somehow, even when their conversion is late, the patterns, the teachings, the early discipline, all seem to jell and take effect at the time of conversion.

SIN IN SCHOOL

I have said that pagan schools do not take sin into account. Christians must do so. Let us consider only one or two of the many ramifications of taking sin seriously in education.

First, teachers are sinners teaching sinners. For the sake of simplicity, we will consider both to be saved sinners. Both are in the process of growing (II Pet. 3:18). Neither is pefect. That means that the relationships that teacher and students, students and students, and teacher and teacher sustain at close range, for long hours five days a week (incidentally, this period of time is not sacred), are bound to get rocky from time to time. All of the biblical principles of confrontation and confession, treated fully in my books on counseling, are operative for the school context. Teachers will teach as much (positively or negatively) by the way they handle their own relationships with students and the examples they set in their relationships with administrators and fellow teachers as in any other ways. They must also help students to grapple with the problems that sin occasions in human relationships toward their peers, other teachers, and their parents. The atmosphere for teaching will be entirely different when teachers regularly handle such matters well.

"Should a teacher ever seek forgiveness of a student or a class?"

Of course.

"Won't he lose authority by doing so?"

Definitely not. He will gain it. In no other way that I know will the genuineness of his own beliefs be so clearly demonstrated to the student.

Students know that teachers sin—they are often on the receiving end of that sin! Also, they have heard the teacher quote the verse "all have sinned." Students reason, easily enough, "That includes him!" Students also know that the teacher tells them to seek forgiveness of others whom they have wronged. "Now," they ask, "does he really believe all of this?" The student will soon find out by the way in which the teacher handles his own sin. Indeed, not only is the teacher's authority as a consistent, genuine Christian leader established by confession of sin, but—of greater importance—Christ's authority over him is established too.

Sin also affects learning. Wise teachers, like wise parents, do not plow on oblivious to obvious problems that are adversely affecting children. They take time to confront, offer counsel, encourage, and help. The Christian school must provide time for such matters, and teachers must be willing and able to spend time attending to them. They must never be mere academes. The day of the impersonal, professional, subject-oriented teacher soon must pass. But more on that later.

The school must anticipate and recognize sin as sin when it occurs. There must be consistent, biblical procedures for dealing with sin, known and adopted by all teachers, and spelled out to all students and parents ahead of time. A child should know what is expected of him in such situations, and how his teacher will deal with sin.

Discipline is a matter of such great importance that a separate book must be devoted to it. But, again, all discipline must be biblically based, procedures must be known to all ahead of time, and agreed upon, and must be carried out according to agreement.

So, the raw product with which Christian educators must work has a basic capacity for education in occupying and controlling tasks, but this capacity has been severely distorted by sin. The raw product is of two grades: regenerate, unregenerate. One is able to do God's will, but not always willing; the other is neither. Sin and its consequences, then, must be taken fully into account.

But, so must God. If there is regular prayer by concerned, believing administrators and staff, if the children come from Christian homes that are a part of God's covenant community, if the churches that they attend are Bible-believing, if many of their peers are Christians, if all the school work is oriented toward God, and if the school has an evangelistic thrust, there is every reason to expect that a finished product comparable to that

63

which is desired may be turned out in the majority of the cases. The Christian school is a place where sin and its consequences are taken into account, but it is also a place where God dwells and is at work. He is given full weight!

But only as that double perspective remains clear in the minds of every responsible person at the school can the dynamic potential of the situation be fully appreciated. Only then will discouragement, sterile traditions, professionalism and other evils be overcome. The school is itself a changing battlefield on which dramatically shifting events take place. Every day new skirmishes occur; some days there are full-scale battles. There are victories and defeats. But, regardless of what any given day may hold, over all there will be advances and many great blessings when we understand these facts, prepare well for warfare and draw upon the limitless resources of God. Success in this internal warfare will lead to graduates who are ready to fight that greater war that looms on the horizon.

9

MOVING FROM RAW PRODUCT
TO FINAL PRODUCT

If the final product of Christian education ought to be a person who thinks and acts like Jesus Christ while pursuing the occupying and controlling activities in which he is engaged, and the raw product is a sinner made in God's image, who may or may not be regenerate, then we must ask, "How do we move from this raw product (A) to that final Product (C)?"

Obviously, in any given case, we cannot move from point A to point C unless, somewhere in the process, the student in view becomes a Christian (if he was not already). When we discussed this issue earlier, we noted the necessity for effective, ongoing evangelism in every Christian school. While I shall say no more about this matter, and in subsequent chapters I shall assume that the school is working largely with Christian students, I do not want to convey the impression thereby that evangelism is either secondary or unimportant. Quite the contrary is true. Biblically speaking, it is fair to say that Christian education truly begins for a student only when he is saved: "the fear of the Lord is the *beginning* of wisdom." Indeed, because the matter is so important, it requires more space than can be given to it in an initial survey such as this; an entire book on evangelism in the Christian school ought to be written. Having said this, we must turn to other things.

At this point I want to survey briefly the process that we will be discussing in detail for the rest of the book, comparing and contrasting it with what now exists in Christian schools.

Look at our Christian schools! They are almost Xerox copies of the school down the street. They hold classes the same number of days per week and meet in buildings that, when money is available, are constructed exactly like those that house their humanistic counterparts; they have a curriculum that approximates the public school curriculum point for point (with perhaps a Bible course or two added); they divide students into grades and classes; they study subjects in classrooms, use textbooks (often the same ones), give tests and final exams, assign homework exercises, grade, pass and fail students, etc. The two look—and even smell—alike! There just isn't much difference.

THE ACE PROGRAM

To be fair, I must point out the fact that there has been one significant innovation on the part of Christian educators. The ACE (Accelerated Christian Education) program does provide a type of learning that uses booklets called PACES, which children study and fill out, and on which they are tested. This approach allows students to proceed at their own rate (an essential for students of differing abilities), and provides individual help to students who are experiencing difficulties. When this help is given in the way that it is supposed to be, students do not tend to fall hopelessly behind as they so frequently do in the more classical formats; they learn to study on their own, the curse of homework is lifted (all work is done in school), and they are not forced to compete with other students. And, it must be said, these PACES have been designed to teach Christian truths and values, and to provide something more distinctively Christian than courses in many other Christian schools. ACE uniforms and other accouterments turn some kids off, but most learn to adapt to them with little trouble. There are some doctrinal problems for some parents and children.

But ACE schools, again, follow the same *basic* curriculum; they also operate in classroom buildings (though some of these buildings remind one more of the old one-room schoolhouse than the modern school plant) and do many other things that closely follow traditional patterns. There are some hopeful signs in these innovations, but they do not go far enough.[1] Like traditional schools, the ACE system does not penetrate deeply enough into the problems of education to the basic issues. Nevertheless, we ought to be thankful to the ACE people for providing an alternative that allows Christians to break out of some of the older molds in which education is formed. This program perhaps is a wedge that God has used to open a crack in the educational world that can be

---

1. Many teachers in conventional schools scoff at the ACE program largely because (1) they are unfamiliar with it, (2) they have heard and bought gossip about it, and (3) it challenges and threatens classical concepts of teaching and of teachers. Some of those teachers who scoff could learn a lot from a serious study of a good ACE school. I am grateful for the ACE program, and in lieu of anything better, I have sent some of my own children 25 miles away every day to attend one. We have seen better results than traditional Christian schools have been able to produce.

widened enough to drive even larger educational innovations through. That is my hope.[2]

Now, in contrast to the fundamental sameness of the Christian educational programs and those of the world, what is it that I am proposing? A sweeping reevaluation of everything! Nothing must be omitted in that reevaluation. I propose that the presuppositions and the goals that we have been considering be turned loose on the process of educating our children to do whatever they must to bring it into complete harmony with biblical principles and practices. I propose that we cease doing anything the way we do it simply because (1) that's the way we've always done it, (2) that's what is expected of a teacher, school or administrator, (3) that's the academic way, (4) that's the way to be respectable, or (5) that's the way it's done down the street. Instead, it is time to ask, "What do biblical presuppositions about the raw and the final products, about teaching methodology, and about every other matter require?"

As an overview, let me reproduce an editorial that I wrote in *The Journal of Pastoral Practice* (4, 4:1-8).

Editorial:

CHRISTIAN EDUCATION IN BIBLICAL PERSPECTIVE

I am anxious to write at length about the subject of Christian education. You may see a book in a year or two. But whether I shall do so or not, here I do wish to express my very deep concern for a reconsideration of the most basic factors underlying what, in many ways, is one of the most important and strategic efforts in which God's people are engaged—Christian education.

Even the most casual survey of the history of modern Christian education shows plainly that Christian schools, on all levels, are little more than spruced up adaptations of the pagan schools down the block. The presuppositions, goals, objectives, methods, curricula, subject areas, materials, etc., with very little (and usually very superficial) change, have been brought over and Christianized. The trouble is that something that in all of its essentials is still at bottom fundamentally pagan cannot be transformed by Christianizing it. Paganism festooned with Christian accouterments is paganism still. Decking out Christian schools with prayer, Bible reading, a Bible course or two, Christian

---

2. It is also my hope that ACE will consider this book and incorporate its teachings into its program.

slogans ("All truth is God's truth"; "We must learn math for God's glory") will not do the trick. These ornaments, as desirable as they may be, are simply that; their presence, no more than the presence of teachers who themselves are Christians, can never transform pagan education into something else. The very presence of a Bible course itself argues against the idea that the rest of the curriculum is Christian; why does the school find it necessary to study the Bible if in all its classes the biblical perspective is being taught? Bible teaching, as such, can be taught by the church and the home; such teaching is not uniquely a school function. Bible courses, in most cases, are an appendage that is deemed necessary because the rest of the curriculum doesn't really do the job. There is a place for teaching the Bible in Christian education, but that place is in the teaching of *every* subject. No, we have tried long enough to do Christian education in the way I have just described—and have failed. So much seems perfectly clear to me; don't you agree?

"Perhaps. But what may be done to change all of this and to enable us to really begin to educate in a manner that is fully Christian? Now that we have a massive, professionalized Christian school movement on our hands (someone recently said that a new Christian school is being organized every seven hours), is it too late to make any significant changes? Who wants to rock the boat by making large waves, as you are suggesting?" you may say. You have a point. But there is hope: all is not lost. Let me explain.

All over America I have talked with Christian school teachers and administrators who feel cheated. They tell me that they entered the field of Christian education with great expectations that have not been realized. They had hoped to be involved in something dramatically different from the education that the world doles out, but in this they have become disappointed and disillusioned. Better than anyone else, they know that, basically, with very few exceptions, what they are doing is not all that different from what their counterparts down the street are doing day by day. They are thankful for Christian fellowship, freedom to talk about Christ, to pray, to use the Scriptures and many other such things, which do create a far more wholesome atmosphere, but they yearn for *more,* something more that will enable them to do what they thought they were going to do—give their classes a truly wall-to-wall, ceiling-to-floor, Christian education. They know that there must be something—indeed a lot—more that they could do for them if they only knew how. Often, they do not even know how to articulate this concern, and those who do, know nothing about where to find help. It is about this something more that I wish to speak in the present editorial.

That it is even thought of as something *more* betrays the fallacy in thinking that pervades so much of the Christian education that we see around us. The kind of transformation of education about which I am speaking cannot be brought about by *adding* something to pagan education. It is that sort of mentality that has brought us into the dilemma in which we now find ourselves. No, it is exactly not something more— adding Christian trappings to essentially pagan offerings—that we must have; rather, it is *something different* that we must have. This something different must be different through and through, from stem to stern. But to attain it we must be willing to do many radical, hard things. We must face formidable obstacles from the Christian world as well as from non-Christians. We must spend hours of laborious thought and effort creating it for the first time ever.

And, we must go back to the basics and begin again. We must ask, ''What are the biblical presuppositions about the purpose of education for life? About teaching? About learning? etc.'' Presuppositions underlie and direct all that we do, whether we are aware of them or whether we can consciously assert them or not. Because so many pagan presuppositions underlying modern education have not been identified by Christians, they have failed to understand why the additive approach is untenable. These must be etched out for all to see, and their biblical alternatives must be compared and contrasted with them. The biblical presuppositions that should govern all that is done in Christian education have never been located and systematically set forth for Christian educators to consider. Until this is done, we will get nowhere; all attempts to transform Christian education into something different will founder.

In determining how to go, questions like these must be answered: Who should be educated? Should Christian education be restricted to believers and to their children? And of these, should all of them be educated or only those who are intellectually capable of going on to college? What does the raw product of Christian education look like? The fact that man is a sinner, for instance, must be given full consideration because it is bound to have wide-ranging implications for teaching and for curricula. How does the fact of sin affect methodology? Pagan schools will not admit the concept of sin into educational theory and therefore have not investigated these all-important matters. The Christian school must pursue every implication of this and every other biblical insight about man to the fullest; we dare not fail to take such factors into account. What are the implications of sinfully caused error and of regeneration or the lack of it for education? These, and dozens of similar questions like them, are of the utmost significance and we must not fail to consider them (yet that is exactly what we have done for the most part). Theology can never be divorced from education. It becomes the basis for a Christian presuppositional pad from which to launch any seriously Christian educational project. But, up until the present, where has theology played any significant part in Christian education? As a matter of fact, most Christian teachers have so little theological knowledge that they are almost totally unable to think about Christian education presuppositionally. We need classes in churches and at the school itself to help to systematically educate teachers in the fundamentals of the faith and their practical implications so that they can begin to think theologically about the work that God has called them to do.

I have mentioned the differences between the regenerate and the unregenerate. The Bible teaches that each will respond to truly Christian approaches quite differently (cf. I Cor. 2). What impact should that fact have on the goals and purposes of Christian education? Surely, this important fact can no longer be ignored as it has been in the past. Expectations, methods of evaluation, and even content will be affected by this all-important distinction. Pagan educators, denying any such distinction, have not grappled with the impact of the fact on education. To bring about a transformation in Christian education we must give the closest attention to the matter. But again, this is virgin territory that will take time and effort to explore.

The fact that a human being is in the image of God, that this image is affected by the fall and again by regeneration must be taken into consideration. The matter of the biblical concept of the heart—the hidden inner life of man that he lives before God and himself—as the source of all outer behavior, including learning, may not be bypassed. And the place of the Holy Spirit and His sanctifying renewal of the mind in the educational process is another vital area that lies virtually untouched. Pious platitudes about spirituality will not get the job done; rather, what is needed is a thoroughly biblical analysis of all of these matters as they pertain to the education of students.

70

Consider for a moment the end product of Christian education: what are we educating for? Could the average Christian teacher or administrator tell us and justify his answer from the Scriptures? You know he couldn't. Well, then, what is he doing day by day? Is the answer "Teaching history" adequate? How will you know unless you can sketch a clear picture of what God wants the finished product of the Christian educational enterprise to look like? Do you know what he should look like?

But assume that you do and that you also know what the raw product that you must work with looks like: do you know how to construct a curriculum that will take him from point A (raw product) to point C (finished product) in such a way that all that you do on the trip grows out of and conforms to the Bible? And, of course, the question arises, How does a school that is alive to all of these needs acquire a staff of educators who know all of this and who know how to develop it in their students? Remember, they must be good at theology, at relating it to education on all levels and must know what in a curriculum is mandated directly by the Scriptures and what ways and means must be devised by them always in a way consistent with biblical presuppositions, precepts and principles. That is a tremendous task. Yet, it is all essential to the acquisition of the something different that is sorely needed.

What I am proposing, I hope you will gather, is not something simple. It will require more than the replacement of a few parts. No, this endeavor, if it is to be done properly at all, will demand strenuous effort by persons qualified and trained to do it. Better that it not be attempted at all than that it be done poorly, or partially. It is the design, manufacture and use of a totally new instrument that I am talking about; it cannot be brought into being by tinkering around with modern education as it now exists.

Moreover, in the consideration of any such attempt to transform education through the application of Christian theology to it, the biblical idea that the school is an extension of the home must be allowed to have full play in all that is attempted. That guiding premise may never be forgotten in anything that is done. *Separate* authority was given to the home, to the church, and to the state by God. This is plainly set forth in the Bible. But the school has received no such authority. It is essentially a three-walled institution that cannot stand alone; it shares as its fourth wall the living room of the Christian home.

71

But today, there is no close affinity between the home and the school. We must, therefore, learn how to close the gap (1) through the development of new communication opportunities and methods, (2) in discipline, (3) in teaching and (4) even in the sort of personnel who are selected to function as teachers. Essentially, we must answer in the most practical terms the question, "How can we get the home back into the school and the school back into the home?" Among the many considerations that will have to be faced is the selection of teaching staff on a widely different basis than most of the present teaching qualifications require. Teachers must be appointed not simply because they are competent in a particular subject area, but because, in addition to that, and in addition to their competence in theology, they show promise as parent-teachers. If the familial father/son discipling method, rather than the Greek, head-packing academic model of teaching be accepted as the biblical method (which it is), then we must also consider the ability of the teacher to exemplify (or model) that which he teaches, along with his academic credits. It is, moreover, crucial for him to incarnate the truth that he teaches in life *as a parent would* for his child. He will be, for the first time, genuinely *en loco parentis*.

But, again, that leads to further considerations of importance. If teaching by discipling is fuller than academic teaching because it *demonstrates* how to use truth for God's glory as well as it teaches that truth, if it stresses not merely facts but is concerned about translating truth into life and ministry, then where and how can we teach such things? Clearly a classroom environment, designed and devoted to exercises having to do merely with the acquisition of abstract knowledge, will never do. Plainly, discipling demands a wider scope. It is "teaching to *observe*" (Matt. 28:20), and that means not only lectures and books, but real life situations. That is the kind of teaching that God required in Deuteronomy 6, 11. The world is the classroom for teaching by discipleship. Students will be in contact with adults and with many sectors of life in the process, not merely with their peers in cloistered halls. And motivation will stem not from grades (that evil that teaches students to study for grades rather than for goals and mastery and that has occasioned so many heartaches), but from the desire of the student (and the fellow students who work with him on it) to accomplish some project or task that will really minister to the church, the home, or the community. Specific facts and skills (like the mastery of the multiplication table) will be learned not in the abstract, but in order to equip one to accomplish some task.

Grades, homework (the surest indicator and the clearest admission of the fact that teachers do not now teach in the classroom) and all such practices will not be accepted simply because "we have been doing it that way." They will be reconsidered in the light of biblical presuppositions and principles. Grading one area of life (the academic), as though it were the most important, will be measured (for instance) over against the biblical doctrine of differing gifts and will be discarded.

Evaluation will be made on the basis of knowledge, life and skills *demonstrated* in genuine tasks that are designed to measure it. But, they will be genuine tasks, not tasks merely contrived to provide another type of (outdoor) exercise.

Individual gifts will be sorted out in the process of assigning tasks for completing projects. Rather than jam everyone into the same curriculum, heedless of the differences that God has built in each student, these projects will train each one for the calling for which God has gifted him. The doctrine of gifts will be taken seriously.

Homework will be dispensed with and parents once again will be allowed time in the evenings to freely enjoy their children. Parents will render significant help to teachers, who should do nothing that a parent could do equally well, lifting many of the burdens that they now bear so that one day a week will be freed up for teachers to plan, study, evaluate, etc. Like their students, teachers will no longer be forced to carry school work home to interfere with their home life and come between them and their husbands, wives and/or children. Parents will teach many skills that are not now offered in Christian schools, but that are required for the accomplishment of specific projects. Projects will not only be designed to teach and to evaluate essential learning while achieving real ends that honor God by blessing others, but they will also be designed around the gifts and skills that God has provided among the parents as well as among the teachers who are a part of a given school. Because of their nature, some will be repeatable from year to year, but many will not. This change will create newness, excitement, and a sense of expectation for all concerned, and will tend to eliminate some of the dullness and the routine that is often connected with teaching. Projects also will make an impact on the community for Christ.

But all of this—and much more—can be achieved only if we become serious about Christian education to a degree that has not yet been known among us. If we do, I am confident that we can turn out a generation of Christians in the near future who in every way will excel those who now graduate from our institutions. They will be equal to every task to which Jesus Christ may call them. But if we do, Christian education will look, smell, taste, sound and feel different from education down the street in nearly every respect; and it will outdistance it at every point as well. How can I say this with such assurance? Because God's way is always superior. And that is what I am calling for—a radical return to biblical practices based on biblical presuppositions and principles. That cannot fail to produce a superior product.

Ah, but who is willing? Who has the courage to begin? What we need are a few schools with the vision that will run pilot programs. I am convinced that to persuade others of the feasibility of the program and of its superiority, we too must use the discipleship method—we must *demonstrate* it to them.

These schools should select a few good teachers who have caught the vision and who are enthusiastic to turn it into a reality, offer this program to a few interested families who, like them, want their children to be trained this way, and over a five-year period (two years for design and three for development and demonstration) effect it. During that time the wrinkles can be ironed out of the program and, at the end, the school will have something to compare and contrast with its regular program. I suggest that either the three years of junior high or the four years of high school (in a six-year pilot program) be allocated to this experiment in biblical education. Perhaps it should be done simultaneously in both at different institutions.

I am personally looking for several schools that would care to help me as I seek to help them to work out these ideas in depth. I shall be anxious for pastors and other readers of the *JPP* to contact school administrators and have them, in turn, contact me if they are interested in working together on such a program. But don't write unless you are serious about it. I have no time for curiosity seekers or for those who do not initially respond with enthusiasm to what I have just written. If this sounds a buzzer inside of you, let me know.—J.E.A.

From this editorial, you will see that there are many things to be considered and much to be done. I shall now take up in more depth each matter mentioned or discussed in the editorial.

10

A THREE-WALLED ENTERPRISE

Christian education for too long has been conducted on the unbiblical principle that education is a task to be assigned to a self-appointed caste of administrators and teachers who belong to an institution that can stand alone as such. This principle has led to many of the current evils of professionalism that have been transferred lock, stock and barrel from the school down the street to the Christian school. The emphasis on academics rather than on discipleship, the arrogant attitude of some teachers and administrators toward parents and children, and the molding of Christian day schools in the shape of prep schools, which chew up and spit out children—children of the covenant—who don't fit that mold, are only a few of these evils of which I speak.

HOME EDUCATION

Let it be said now, clearly and plainly: the school, even the Christian school, has no reason for a separate existence of its own. God has not ordained that it should stand alone; it is always to be considered a three-walled, rather than a four-walled, enterprise.

Clearly, in the Scriptures, God speaks of several well-defined spheres of activity to which separate authorities are given. There is the family (the most basic), the church, the state, and business. All of these regularly get separate treatment at various places in the Bible, in both the Old and the New Testaments. But nowhere—in neither the Old Testament nor the New Testament—is the school accorded a sphere or an authority of its own. Indeed, in the Bible the school is not even considered an institution. It is this institutionalization of the school as a separate entity, distinct from the home, from the church, from the state, and from business, that has caused many of the difficulties that this book is designed to alleviate.

What do I mean when I say that, biblically speaking, the Christian school is a three-walled enterprise? I am trying to communicate, under a figure of speech, an important truth that is fundamental to all that is done in truly Christian education: schooling, in God's sight, must never be an independent, but, rather, a dependent, enterprise. A school has no life of its own. Strictly speaking, there should be no "school"; only schooling. The word "school" occurs only once in the Bible (Acts 19:9), where it speaks of a Greek, not a Christian, school. Christian schooling is dependent on one of the other authority spheres and is an activity that comes under its authority.

General education is a function of the Christian home. While each of the other spheres has a teaching task appropriate to its functions to pursue, it is not the fundamental, foundational teaching for all of life that is learned in business, in the church (which doesn't teach language, math, etc.), or in the service of the state. Business teaches what is essential to the pursuit of the trade that one follows (e.g., tentmaking), and business is often subsumed under the home (the two are not necessarily separate). The state may properly teach law, government, the way to use force, and such other functions as are essential to the maintenance of law and order. And the church teaches the Bible and biblical principles of loving God and man that are to be used in every sphere of life. It also teaches the home how to inculcate these very same principles, and exhorts the home, the state, and the business world to live according to them.

The entire witness of the Scriptures, then, is that general education is a function of the Christian home. The fourth wall of the Christian school is the living room of the Christian home. In the Bible, the two are connected, and it is at the peril of all concerned—teachers, children, and parents—that a fourth wall has been erected. Ripping the school away from the home and attempting to give it a separate existence by throwing up a flimsy fourth wall, contrary to God's blueprints, has created a dangerous dichotomy between the school and the home. Both have suffered as a result. The whole building is in danger of collapsing on children and teachers alike.

Christian school properly is an extension of the Christian home. The gap that now exists between the school and the home is disastrous and is one of the major causes of what has become known as the generation gap. The school gap is behind many of the tensions and strains that are pulling the home apart. It tends to set children and parents apart into two separate camps, each existing in a distinct world of its culture and influence. It is a major source of juvenile crime and violence. It contributes, more than any other factor, to the delinquency that is found among so many children today. And, while the problem is somewhat lessened in some Christian schools, that is by no means universally the case.

If we are ever going to establish Christian education on a proper base, we must tear down that wall and rebuild our schools as a part of the home itself. But, were we to do so, even then we would find that the door between the classroom and the living room is tightly locked. Teachers and parents occasionally (in formal ways) slide notes ("Dear Mrs. Jones," "Dear Parent") and report cards back and forth beneath the door, but they themselves rarely venture through it. In this chapter I want to talk about how to find and use the key to that door.

But first, let us briefly examine (an entire book someday must be written concerning this theme) some evidence for placing Christian education in the sphere of the home rather than in one of the other God-given spheres.

As we have seen, Scripture provides no God-given authority to the school; it does not institutionalize the school as such. There is no command to begin a school, to attend a school, or to obey the authority of school teachers. There is an authority/submission structure set up between parents and children, church officers and members, husbands and wives, employers and employees, the state and its citizens. The authority of a school or an independent school teacher over pupils is unknown to the Bible.

There are, however, many commands to teach, and there is much about teachers. These commands are given to fathers, parents, and the families of Israel. Some of the most prominent commands are found in Deuteronomy 4, 6, and 11. The principal words used in these contexts are *yadah* ("to perceive, to see, to cause to know"), *lamad* ("to teach, to discipline, to train"), and *shanan* ("to sharpen, to whet, to repeat"[1]). The father is specifically singled out as the one finally responsible for inculcating the essential knowledge that his child must have. Mothers, and other family members, however, are commended for their efforts in teaching children as well (cf. II Tim. 1:5; Titus 2:3-5).

Elsewhere Levites are said to teach (II Chron. 35:3; Neh. 8:9), but the word *bin* ("to separate, to distinguish, to cause to understand, to ex-

---

1. The presence of acrostic psalms and other mnemonic devices shows the concern for teaching by rote memorization and by repetition of the truth. The repeated action of rubbing the blade against a stone in whetting the sword is involved in the imagery of the word.

plain, to interpret'') is used to describe the *expository role* that was assigned to them. Their teaching was interpretation of the Bible rather than training children to live according to it in ordinary life situations.

There are intimations of teaching by more teachers than one, and probably teachers other than parents (see Ps. 119:99: "all my teachers" or "those teaching me"; here *lamad* is used); and mothers and older *women* are said to teach (Prov. 31:1; Titus 2:3-5); rulers, prophets, and scribes teach the people generally, but are not said to engage in individual training.

The so-called "schools of the prophets" (II Kings 2:3ff.; 4:38f.) do not seem to have been schools at all. The Bible never uses the word "school" with reference to them, but, as Meyer says, they seem to have been "associations or brotherhoods," guilds established for "mutual edification"[2] rather than for educational purposes (though in II Kings 4:38 the phrase "sitting before him" possibly could be construed as a discipling context. Cf. Acts 22:23[3]).

There are interesting indications of general literacy, which was taught by parents. A child's (*any* child's) early writing ability had become proverbial (Isa. 10:19). In Isaiah 29:11-12, we are told that the inability to understand God's revelation prevailed universally so that asking for an explanation of it was like attempting to read a sealed scroll. Neither those who could read and write (the "learned" ones) nor those who couldn't (the "unlearned" ones) could do so. Learning (literacy) made no difference; ignorance of God's Word was universal. Here the distinction between some who were literate and some who were not is made. Plainly, though training in reading and writing was widespread, it was not mandatory, and therefore not universal. Josephus says that the law

> commands us to bring those children up in learning, and to exercise them in the laws, and make them acquainted with the acts of their predecessors, in order to their imitation of them, and that they might be nourished up in the laws from their infancy, and might neither transgress them, nor have any pretense for their ignorance of them.[4]

---

2. H. H. Meyer, "Education," *I.S.B.E.*, (Grand Rapids: Eerdmans, 1949), 2:901.

3. Clearly, promising students were sent to study under outstanding leaders for discipling or apprenticeship in becoming a prophet (I Sam. 1:24-28) or rabbi (Acts 22:3) or for learning a trade from those skilled in it (Exod. 35:34). In two of the three instances I have mentioned the training was on an advanced level that would correspond to our college work or beyond.

4. *Against Apion*, II:26.

According to Meyer (op. cit.) the "learning" of which Josephus writes is the rudiments of reading and writing. It seems evident, then, that since God gave a written revelation to His people, they prized reading and writing and that parents taught these skills to their children so that they could understand God's law. After all, it was written on the doorposts, on the city gates, etc., for the general citizenry to read and recall (Deut. 6:8, 9). A written revelation led to the fact of a general literacy.

The biblical evidence, though meagre, is plain: biblical education was three-walled. And even when a child was sent off to obtain greater knowledge or skills from a tutor or craftsman, it was not to an institutionalized school that he went but to one individual (or to individuals) who acted in the place of a parent and assumed a discipling (i.e., parental) relationship to him. The responsibility for general education was assumed by neither the state, nor the church, nor the business community; it was the home that undertook to educate in accordance with God's commands.[5] This fact is of great importance to our study.

Now, we must turn to what is the heart of our concern in this chapter. We have discovered that the Christian school is a responsibility of the home, that a child's teaching and training is a parental activity, and that it is only when greater knowledge or skills than those possessed by the parents themselves are required that the child was sent to a tutor or craftsman, who acted as a parent to the child.[6] Given these facts, and in view of what we have today, we can only say that it is time to

BRING THE HOME BACK INTO THE SCHOOL

As the following chapters develop, I shall explain in greater detail exactly how this may be done. But for the present my concern is to set forth the general principles for turning Christian education once again into a parental rather than a professional enterprise. Along the way, nevertheless, I shall make a number of concrete suggestions.

---

5. We are told, "Education was widely diffused; the mass of the people were able to read and write. The sons of rich houses had their tutors; parents of more modest circumstances taught their own children." Later on (A.D.98–117), synagogs had Bible schools for "the study of tradition—al lure," and teachers had to be married, but schools were organized "in all towns and villages" only as late as A.D. 225–255. Cf. Margolis and Marx, *A History of the Jewish People* (Philadelphia: The Jewish Pub. Society of America, 1927), pp. 88, 210, 211, 225.

6. Cf. Eli's parental address to Samuel as "my son" (I Sam. 3:6, 16). Of course, in this case there were unique circumstances.

To begin with, parents must recognize that in sending a child to Christian school they are surrendering to the teacher full parental authority over the child. He or she truly is *en loco parentis* ("in the place of a parent"). That old Latin phrase comes from a time when society recognized this principle. But actually only Christian teachers of a proper sort, doing what God commands, can properly discharge the duties thus entrusted to them. This is *full* parental authority, not merely the right to convey information and repackage heads. The student is a whole person, living in and reacting as a whole person to a whole environment. The teacher, therefore, must have full parental authority during the hours the child is under his discipleship to guide him and respond to him on all levels. He must be allowed to show full concern for the student as a total person. Because education is parental, authority must be total; because education is total, authority must be parental.

Parents must be taught this fact when they enroll their children in a Christian school, should be fully informed about the implications of it, and must intelligently assent to it. They must be encouraged to let Christian teachers counsel, train, discipline, and teach values, beliefs, habits, and attitudes as well as facts about mathematics, history, etc. They must recognize that at school the teacher and their child are in an Ephesians 6:1-4 relationship.

On the other hand, teachers must *assume* this full authority and responsibility. The biblical model is discipleship in which the pupil *becomes* (not just "thinks") like his teacher (Luke 6:40). He must recognize the sweeping implications of this truth and be prepared to enter into all of them. The discipleship model (seeing and hearing) is a *parental* model that is founded on the Father-Son relationship of Jesus, God's *Son,* and God His *Father* (cf. John 8:38-44; 5:19, 20, 30; 3:32).

So, it is clear that more than content is taught in schooling. The academic model (teaching of content alone), practically speaking, is impossible to follow; both teachers and students are whole persons who (whether they know it or not) communicate and receive communications about all sorts of things on all levels all the time. The academic ideal, therefore, is unattainable and deceiving, and its pursuit is fraught with futility. Teachers cannot *avoid* teaching values and beliefs explicitly as well as implicitly—even when they try.[7] The biblical, discipleship

7. Indeed, to try to do so reveals one's values about values, etc.

model takes cognizance of this important fact and, as its genius, *capital-izes* on it! Recognition of the fact leads to many important practices such as selecting teachers not merely on the basis of academic knowledge and ability, but also on the basis of their beliefs, personalities, lifestyles, and parental qualities. That is why, for instance, a Christian school may not hire a known homosexual.

Teachers themselves must make every effort to show love for children, be good examples for them, and be able to offer wise counsel to them. And they must be willing to cooperate smoothly with parents in the training of their children. Consistency in discipline at home and at school is necessary, and unbroken communication between the two must be maintained at all times. Both parent and teacher will want this when both consider themselves *parental teachers,* one of whom happens to be at home *emphasizing* parenting and the other at school *emphasizing* teaching. And each must recognize the other as such.

When this recognition exists, there will be a willingness and a desire to exchange any and all information that is significant either to parenting or to teaching. There will be none of the dichotomizing of the two roles that the phrase ''parent-teacher meeting'' conjures up in our minds. Parental teaching at school will be seen by all as an extension of the educational parenting that is done at home.

The door between the living room and the classroom must be un-locked, and the key thrown away!

There should be many substantive evaluative conferences between parents, children, and teachers; report cards are too impersonal. The quarterly report card is, in a sense, a symbol of the lack of communica-tion that exists between the home and the school. It gives parents numbers or letters, but very little information about what, exactly, a child knows or can do, and virtually nothing about his Christian character.

Note, in these evaluative conferences the child should be present. Unlike the usual parent-teacher conference, which so easily may become a gossip session about children, these conferences will assure the child that his presence is desired. When all are present, explanations can be made with all data available (cf. Prov. 18:17), and commitments made will be understood by all parties. And, what is of equal significance, everyone will know that everyone knows everything.

There must be such good communication between the home and the school that if, for instance, there is serious illness at home or the death of a close relative, the parental teacher in the school may treat the child accordingly, recognizing that this crisis may greatly affect his performance.

In order to achieve this sort of communication, it will be necessary to bring parents into the school milieu itself. They must be able not only to review the results of the projects in which their children have been engaged, but also to see them engaged in these projects. And, at times, they too will help out in such projects. Also, using parents for field trip guides, study period monitors, record keepers, etc., in short, engaging them to do anything and everything that they can do *as well as* the teacher himself, not only will relieve teachers of many unnecessary burdens that now make teaching a chore, but will free teachers for tasks that parents cannot perform, and will occasion a healthy mix of parents and teachers that is conducive to good communication.

A parent from each home, in entering his children, must agree to spend a prescribed number of hours each month in some way aiding teachers to instruct his child. This agreement must be made a prerequisite for acceptance.[8] All of which brings us to the second fact: If it is time to bring the home back into the school, it is also time to

BRING THE SCHOOL BACK INTO THE HOME

"What on earth could you mean by that?" you ask.

Just what I said.

"But you don't mean that literally, do you?"

Yes.

Clearly this is the more radical proposal of the two, and it will have the more visible effects. If we have failed anywhere, it is here. There have been feeble, token attempts to bring parents to school. The open house night, in which teachers often are carefully insulated from all significant one-to-one contact with parents, is one good example. But virtually nothing has ever been done to bring students and teachers into homes.

---

8. While this may create some difficulties among working mothers, this prerequisite (1) makes parents consider priorities, and (2) demands creative responses by both school and home to overcome the problems. Some of these difficulties will be resolved by later proposals, such as opening one's home or business to the school for various purposes. Parents each year must agree also to take a brief course of instruction about maintaining communication and cooperation between the home and the school.

Professionalizing Christian education, setting it off sharply from the home, has driven far from our minds the thought of using Christian homes as a setting for a part of a child's education. The very idea sounds "unprofessional," and thus (to our professionally trained ears) absurd. But think twice about the idea; don't dismiss it out of hand.

We have noted already that, despite report cards, parents are virtually ignorant of what goes on in the Christian school on a day-by-day basis. They pay their tuition, send their children off to school, and that is it. Of course, many parents and many teachers like it that way. But I shall presume that if you have purchased this book and are still reading it, you are one of those who do not. You as a parent know that you have a greater responsibility toward your child, but the present system locks you out of the school so that you can't discharge your responsibility. While it is important to grant full parental authority to teachers, it is also incumbent on you to discover how this authority is exercised, and (at times) to help teachers exercise it better. After all, parent, it is *your children* who are being taught; and the teachers who teach them are *your servants;* PTA and PTF meetings will not do for that purpose. Parents have not been assuming their responsibilities—even in a review capacity. And, they have been expecting the teacher to do too much.

It is not true that parents can do nothing toward the education of their children but pray and pay. It is not true that all of the education that is carried on must be done by a parental teacher. Teaching parents may also add a great deal to the schooling of their children. There are many activities (about which I shall speak in depth, *infra*) in which a parent can share the load with the teacher, thus lightening the load for him.[9]

There are some things that parents can teach better than the school, and some of these can be taught best in homes. Why should all teaching occur at school? As we shall see in a later chapter, teaching must go on in *every* life situation to be fully biblical; and, surely, the home is a significant part of anyone's life. Why, then, can't the home and the school blend what they have to offer?

Parents should become involved in teaching just as teachers must

---

9. I know that some teachers and administrators see inclusion of parents in education as an additional burden. Obviously, it could be a burden if not wisely planned and *would* be so in the present system of things. But this proposal presupposes (1) a new system (yet to be explicated in detail) and (2) both parents and teachers working hard to make it a success. Results will spur both to new heights of cooperation.

become involved in parenting. In no other way can parents really keep up with the progress that their children are making. It is time to close the gap, open the door, erase the artificial line that has been drawn between home and school, between parent and teacher, and move back and forth through the door. There is no such biblical boundary as now exists.

"Well, how shall we do so?"

While any full explanation must await matters that I shall discuss in subsequent chapters, here I shall hazard a *few* (note this word) comments nonetheless.

One of the major problems about which teachers (rightly) complain is that they need more time to do all that they must do. Some of the difficulty arises from foolish paper work and busy work that is done in lieu of any substantial student projects, some from wrong teaching objectives and methods, some from poor habits, and some from the twin curses of homework and grading, but also some from requiring too much of a teacher. I propose not only to eliminate the first five difficulties, but also the sixth—by giving teachers more time.

There are many taped and written materials (and under this program there could be even more) to which children could listen at home or in the school room. Video tape presentations probably should be restricted to the school for some time to come, until home video equipment is as widespread as TV. There is no reason why a teacher must sit in on periods of reading, audio tape listening, etc. Perhaps a full day could be devoted to such activities which could be conducted in various homes in the community. It is possible that on that day no one (including teachers) need come to school. This, by the way, could lead to great financial savings for the school (light, heat, etc.), and even smaller savings for some homes (travel and lunch). Parents can easily monitor periods of reading, listening, writing, etc. Simple, mechanical evaluations of work, according to prepared keys, also could be done by parents rather than by teachers. And, to the extent that tests will be retained, these too can be taken at home. [10] And, what better way is there for parents to keep well informed about their children's progress?

Then, there are all of the home economics and shop-type activities

---

10. There will be no problem with parents cheating; cheating will not be possible since knowledge, life and skill for use (*however* acquired) will be the goal, not grades (see *infra*). I do not advocate graded tests. Any tests that are retained should be check-ups, given for the sake of the student, not in order to grade him.

(not courses or exercises, as you will see presently) that will be *necessary* for learning skills and for pursuing various projects (also to be explained later) that will be a part of truly Christian education. Many of these activities could be done best in homes—in basement shops and sewing rooms. Moreover, credit should be given for supervised chores and projects that may be done *at* home *for* the home (or church, for that matter). Because of the energies and time presently devoted to *exercises* at school, parents and the church get little mileage out of their children. Exercises are substituted for *real work.*

Indeed, these are but a few suggestive *thrusts;* they do not constitute a *program.* And, as I have been intimating, there is much more yet to be discussed to demonstrate exactly how, in these and in numerous other ways, parents can become deeply involved—according to their gifts and proper priorities—in some phases of their children's education.

If we were to erase the artificial boundary line between the school and the home, and begin to involve parents seriously, it is my opinion that we could provide a four-day teaching week (or its equivalent) for each teacher. That would leave a full day's worth of time for preparation—the time teachers have been looking for. This extra day would free them up at nights, so that they would not find it necessary to take work home. Actually, it is sinful for schools to require teachers to do so, thus destroying family and social life. Moreover, it would put parents and children back together during the most productive part of their day. One of the problems, at present, is the way that the school comes between parent and child. More than anything I know, this has led to the deterioration of family life.

The sterile professionalism of most schools (and I know that parents and teachers often like it that way) tends to militate against any real communication, understanding, cooperation, and fellowship. That must be changed.

So much at this point for this point. As I said, what I have talked about in this chapter is not a program, but merely a series of thrusts. The program must be developed. In various places, it may develop in different ways. But the biblical thrusts made here are needed and, in one way or another, must be fully unpacked if we are ever to see truly Christian education in our midst.

11

TRUTH, LIFE AND MINISTRY

THE HOLY SPIRIT IN EDUCATION

The place of the Holy Spirit in Christian education is hardly ever considered. Indeed, on reading the subheading of this introductory paragraph you may have been taken aback by the very idea of the Holy Spirit in education—the words are so unfamiliar! Oh, now and then, reference to the Holy Spirit may be made, but when you consider what is actually done in the programing and in the day-by-day operation of even a school that is strongly committed to Christian education, I think you must admit that, for all practical purposes, the Holy Spirit might not even exist.

Apart from the personal devotion of individual Christian teachers and administrators (and, I admit that God uses this—often powerfully), there's little dependence on the Holy Spirit and His work for teaching and learning. The present fundamental structure of education, borrowed as it is from a pagan, humanistic model that has no place for God and sees no need for him, allows for no way to change the situation. And, in it, there is no concern for such change. Indeed, a few might even consider talk about the Holy Spirit "unprofessional." To those caught up in the many evils of professionalism, I can understand how it is quite so. Nothing will shatter professionalism more thoroughly than earnest, prayerful dependence on the Holy Spirit by parents and teachers alike; that stance is the very antithesis of humanistic self-sufficiency!

How has this strange divorce of the Holy Spirit and Christian education come about? A major reason for the sort of professionalism that separates God's power from education is the acceptance of the pagan academic model (which comes from Greek thought, and emphasizes truth for truth's sake) which separates truth from life. Akin to that tragic disjunction is a second: the separation of truth from wisdom (or, God's way of viewing and living life[1]). Modern humanistic educators think that

---

1. The Book of Proverbs is an educational treatise. That it seems quite different from modern educational books is understandable; this difference stems not from a cross-

truth can be known (1) apart from God's perspective on life, and (2) apart from living life by the Holy Spirit's power. Both of these errors, working hand in hand, have effectively eliminated the Holy Spirit from the serious thinking and planning even of most Christian educators.

In the Scriptures, the Holy Spirit is called the "Spirit of truth" (John 16:13[2]). It is He who "guided" the apostles into "all truth." Clearly, from these words, one can see that His concern is educational; the Spirit is inextricably involved in the impartation of truth (which is more than knowledge[3]). How, then, can Christian educators, who purport to be in the business of searching out and dispensing truth—and, as a matter of fact, *ought* to be, as they study and seek to obey God's command to occupy and control—fail to take into account the place and the work of the Holy Spirit in education? If truth isn't a central concern of Christian education, then what is?

True Christian education, then, is education that is bound up with sanctification, i.e., growth in one's spiritual life. It is a moral, life-altering experience, not an amoral activity. This education is dependent on repentance and faith that leads to wisdom; it is an education that, through the work of the Holy Spirit, spiritualizes all of life. That is to say, Christian education depends on the Spirit's illumination and application of His Book, the Bible, for the correct perception and relationship of every fact, and on His energizing power for living according to biblical truth in all aspects of life.

WISDOM IN EDUCATION

The principal Hebrew word for wisdom, *chokmah,* which permeates the thought of Old Testament *and* New Testament writers and has given rise to a genre of writing we call "wisdom literature,"[4] denotes *wisdom by experience,* not just by study. It also includes the ideas of discrimination between good and evil, the receiving of instruction, attitude) or mind set), and the exercising of correct judgment and skills. The scope of the word is large, encompassing the totality of one's intellectual, living

---

cultural disjunction; rather this strangeness is due to our lack of familiarity with *wisdom* in education. Wisdom is the combination of fact and the divine interpretation of it for everyday living. Proverbs shows that the acquisition of wisdom, rather than the accumulation of knowledge, is the goal of education.

2. See also John 14:17; 15:26.
3. Truth = knowledge and facts properly interpreted and oriented to life.
4. But it also has influenced all other subsequent biblical writing and thought.

and performing experience. We have no equivalent term in English. Our own word, "wisdom," by contrast, is impoverished.[5] It is a word that, in fact, rapidly seems to be disappearing from our vocabulary. Fundamentally, the biblical word *wisdom* brings together three factors: knowledge, life and ministry. It is knowledge, understood from God's perspective, made profitable for day-by-day living for Him, and (as a part of that) shared with others and used to minister to them.

Added to the more general purposes of education, considered in chapter 6, are these three (knowledge, growth, ministry), to which we also must give consideration.

But, before we do, let me say one word more about truth, and the Spirit of truth in education. The education of a Christian must be considered a part of his sanctification. It involves his relationship to God, to his neighbor, and to the rest of God's creation. It is, therefore, a moral matter to believe or disbelieve a truth; all relationships and all beliefs have a moral dimension. Truth is from God; error and all untruth is from Satan (cf. I John 4:6[b]). While the expression "all truth" in John 16:13 does not have a direct reference to information about how to raise pigs, conduct a business, or construct roads, it does refer to all the biblical truth that is necessary to do these (or any other biblically legitimate) activities in a manner that is pleasing to God and is, therefore, pertinent.

Today, the goals of the occupying/controlling commandment cannot be achieved (apart from the application of the redemptive commandment) as they might have been before the fall. Educators—even Christian ones—have attempted (unsuccessfully) to follow the former commandment as if there had been no fall. But that cannot be done. Doing so leads to legalism, frustration and humanism. For believers, doing so means attempting to become sanctified in this all-important area of life apart from the wisdom and the strength of the Holy Spirit.

The redemptive commandment (Matt. 11) applies not only to justification—that forensic, declarative act of God in salvation—but also to sanctification, that gradual, life-long work of God by which He makes us more and more like Christ while removing more and more sin from our lives. The redemption that lifts crushing burdens and replaces them with

---

5. Formerly, "wisdom," in English, was richer and meant "the whole of practical knowledge"—George Crabb, *English Synonyms* (New York: Harper and Brothers, 1891), p. 82.

Christ's lighter loads, surely has in view more than a judicial pronounce-ment. Indeed, while encompassing the forensic element, the focus of Matthew 11:28-30 is primarily experiential. That is to say, it emphasizes the blessings of sanctification that flow from salvation.

Christian education, rightly pursued, *is* a cause that refreshes. But that refreshment comes only from a vital, spiritual relationship to Christ in which the Spirit is enabling the student to see and to live life God's way (I Cor. 2). Those who are "in the flesh" (i.e., unregenerate persons, who are devoid of the Spirit) cannot please God (Rom. 8:8). That is true of the learned scholar, the shrewd businessman, the rich farmer, or anyone else who is without Christ. The regenerate man (the one to whom the Holy Spirit has given spiritual life) not only *can* please God, but does, in fact, do so. He has been given wisdom (understanding and power) to sanctify all of life to God, if he only will, and thereby to enjoy all the blessings of his new life.

TRUTH, LIFE, AND MINISTRY

What I have been leading up to is this: the Holy Spirit educates differently; He does not educate as the humanists do, or even as Chris-tians who follow humanists do. His educational objective is not merely the acquisition of facts; it is not even the acquisition of truth. He has more in mind: He is concerned about what is done with that truth and what that truth does. His objective is changed lives.

This emphasis surfaces most clearly in that great educational passage, Matthew 28:18-20:

> And Jesus went to them and said to them, "All authority in heaven and on earth has been given to Me. Go, therefore, and make disciples from all nations, baptizing them into the Name of the Father and of the Son and of the Holy Spirit, teaching them to observe all that I have commanded you; and remember, I will be with you always, to the close of the age."

Usually, this passage is referred to as the Great Commission, and it is that, of course. But in making an emphasis on missions, the sturdy educational framework of the passage often has been ignored, or even distorted.

Because, by His death and resurrection, Jesus Christ had been given "all authority in heaven and on earth," He sent out His apostles to recruit students (disciples) from all nations. Those who were saved would be matriculated into His school by baptism, and would thereupon enter into a life-long course of education. It is the description of that educational curriculum with which we presently are concerned: *"teaching* them to *observe* all that I have commanded you." The words "teaching . . . to observe" say it all. Obedient observance of Christ's commandments is the objective of the Holy Spirit's education.

Much needs to be said (elsewhere) about the latter portion of that program ("all I have commanded you"); here our focus must rest strictly on the words "teaching them to observe." Always, biblical discipleship is twofold, in contrast to the more limited academic objective of modern education. Academic teaching today is teaching in the abstract. Facts are individually hung out on the clothesline to dry. They flap in the breeze, unrelated to one another and to life. Biblical (Spirit-energized) education, on the other hand, is education *for life;* it is teaching *to be "observed"* (i.e., put to use in daily living). Dewey spoke of *learning by doing* and was wrong. Christians must speak instead of learning *for* doing, if they are to be right.[6] Truth, in the Scriptures, is never taught for its own sake; it is always taught *for use*. In introducing the letter to Titus, Paul said that God had chosen him to "promote the faith of God's chosen people and the full knowledge of the truth *that brings about godliness"* (Titus 1:1). Truth is for use.[7] That is why one of the Bible's favorite phrases is "walking in the truth."

This biblical concept of *truth for use* means that the academic model ("Here are the facts; learn them and show us that you have on tests") is inadequate. It is, therefore, chilling to hear Christian educators boast about the "academic excellence" of their schools. Whenever I hear such claims, I suspect that those who make them are on the wrong track: the world's track rather than God's.

What *should* Christian educators wish to achieve? Godly living; that is what. All truth—yes, even about pigs, and business, and roads—ought to be so related to Jesus Christ that one is more godly because he has learned it. That will happen only when his learning is *for doing*. Every fact that he acquires must be (1) oriented properly into his Christian

---

6. I shall say more about this later. Dewey's idea was that education was the expression of what was within. Christian education is the living of God's truth in everyday affairs.

7. Later, we shall see how vital this point is in designing a curriculum for schools.

stance toward life, placing God's interpretation on it, and (2) turned into life and ministry.

That is to say, when a student is taught facts, they must be taught from a biblical perspective and fitted into the Christian system. The Christian draws implications for life and ministry (the facts are sanctifying; yes, even facts about pigs and roads, properly applied, can be sanctifying) as he actually integrates truth into daily living. He must be *taught* "to observe," and is *properly* taught, therefore, only when he *learns* to observe. To "observe" means to integrate what one is taught into daily living.

You have noticed that I said facts were to be used for life *and for ministry*. What one has learned, and learned to live, must also be shared; that is an essential part of the "godliness" of which Paul wrote in Titus 1:1 and of the commands of Christ mentioned in Matthew 28. Every blessing received may be shared; every skill learned may be used to be a blessing to others. Every step in sanctification makes one a greater debtor to others. Thus, the proper outcome of education that is truly Christian, in one way or another, must involve truth, life, and ministry.

In conclusion, to those who cannot see how facts about pigs, business or roads can be life-changing and provide occasions for ministry, let me say only this: that is the central problem in your approach to education. Until you can begin to see the spirituality of pig raising as a controlling activity by which God may be glorified, you will never understand what Christian education is all about.

Doubtless, at this point, such statements confuse you. They may seem to be as ethereal as a Platonic world of ideas; but this is no set of abstract platitudes about which I am speaking. I have been talking about "observing" ("keeping" by practicing in life) what one learns—that is precisely the opposite of the abstract, academic approach. It would, therefore, be the epitome of stupidity to do exactly what I am opposed to doing.

Please be patient; I have not yet finished. As you read further, you will see that it is only through a vitally new and revolutionary approach to education that these goals can be concretized. Certainly they sound vague and pietistic when related to the present educational enterprise that we all know so well. But as I begin to outline a radically new approach to education in the chapters that follow, I think you will begin to see that this seemingly idealistic idea of "teaching to observe" is, after all, preeminently practical. I shall be anxious for your response as the whole picture becomes more apparent.

12

THE NEW TEACHER

The new education, about which I have been writing, will be new largely because it will be taught by a new sort of teacher. Apart from a new teacher, a new system will fail; it can be safely said that the two stand or fall together.

This teacher will find his work exciting and extremely rewarding; he will actually be able to *see* the fruit of his labors. Teachers, trained under the old academic model, who have little flexibility, and who jealously hold on to the academic professionalism that is connected with it, will not be able to make the transition to the new education and will never enter into its blessings and benefits.

Teachers who cannot wholeheartedly buy into the basic principles and practices of the new education, and who (therefore) will not really be acceptable to those who sponsor it, will have to find their place in schools where the old views and traditions prevail. There will be plenty of these around, for a long time, I fear; I fully expect traditionalism, even in Christian circles, to die hard. One thing that the new education does not need, however, is teachers who are still committed to the old education. Nor do these teachers need the trouble they will run into if they attempt to function in the new program while still believing in the old. The fundamental antithesis between the two systems is so great that there is no possible way to bridge the gap.

The new education will have a hard road to travel for some time, and it will spread slowly. But, in the end, it will prevail among Christians because it is more biblical. Wherever it is properly adopted, it will bring a new sense of satisfaction to teachers, parents and children alike.[1] But until it is tried successfully in a number of places, it will occasion widespread doubt and skepticism.

Indeed, we shall be told again and again in any number of ways, that this bumblebee cannot fly. It is only when the sound of the bumblebee's

---

1. Of course, because of sin, it will not work perfectly; far from it. But because it takes sin and its effects fully into account, it will overcome problems that arise.

flight, hither and yon, is heard buzzing loudly in their ears that the skeptics will be silenced. Even then they will find fault; and that is understandable because for some time to come there will be plenty of wrinkles in detail to iron out. And whenever sinners do anything—even the right thing—there is always room to find fault. But while picking for flaws, they will conveniently forget the far more serious failures of the academic model to which they so tenaciously cling. They will not promote the new education; rather, they will do all that they can to impede its progress—or so it seems if, in this, the usual course of things prevails.

Because of this, it will be courageous administrators and parents, together with a host of forward-looking teachers, who determine that this is what they and their children must have even at great cost and effort, because it is what God requires. Any lesser motivation will fail because it too would be horizontal—humanistic. The last thing that must take place is to begin this program for humanistic reasons! Nothing would be more thoroughly devastating to its ultimate goals. It will be *persons*, then, who are motivated properly, who will bring about the new era in Christian education that is needed to meet the challenge of humanism. These persons will be alert to the signs of the times.

THE NEW TEACHER

What will the new teacher who becomes such an integral part of this new education look like? Let me, at least in part, draw his/her portrait.

More often than not, this new teacher is in his 30s. He is old enough to have had his fill of, and become thoroughly disillusioned by, Christian school academics, and yet young enough to make the radical changes that will be necessary to become involved. Some older teachers with a large capacity and desire for change also will be among the staunchest advocates of the new education. At first, there will not be many younger teachers. For the most part they will be full of the mythology about teaching that they will have received in college. They will not yet have become disillusioned. But there will be some, with insight and wisdom beyond their years, who from the first will be able to compare and choose. The new teacher, then, will be a mature, forward-looking individual; the new education will be blessed from the outset with teachers from among the pick of the crop.

This new teacher also will be a thinker. He will not accept courses of action because "that's the way it is done." Nor will he abandon that which is good, tried-and-true, simply for novelty's sake. He will study the Bible on his own and reach the conclusion that the new education is, in fact, closer to the biblical picture of education than the old; and he will want to be a part of it *for that reason*. He will be a person, doing what he is doing, out of conviction. He will think presuppositionally, not pragmatically; he will be something of a theologian and an exegete in his own right, and will understand the need for a solid theological base on which to build a Christian educational system.

This new teacher will be a flexible, growing, creative person; he will *have* to be (1) because of the nature of the new education, and (2) because at first he will have to help prepare curricula, etc., from scratch. He will not be one to shy away from such a challenge, but rather will welcome it. He will recognize that he is in on the ground floor of a pioneering effort of great importance and will want to contribute to it all that he can.

He will not let small setbacks discourage him, he will not give up when the going gets tough or when traditionalists criticize or scorn, and he will be anxious to solve problems rather than complain about them. He will not expect to have everything handed to him on a silver platter; he knows that he must innovate—grab hold of biblical principles and run with them. He will enjoy this aspect of teaching. He will help others, will overflow with hope, fired by the conviction that at last he is on the right track—God's track.

This new teacher will be parental. He will revel in working with children. He will love them and care about them as if they were his very own. He will want to help them grow as Christians, not only intellectually, but spiritually. He will be conscious of the need to set an example for them by his life and conduct; he will disciple them, when necessary, counseling and encouraging them along the rough spots in the road. His relationship to them will be more than "professional."

This new teacher will be a model not only of someone lecturing about his subject (there will be much less of that anyway), but also of one who, himself, *does* what he talks about. He will develop ways and means of letting students look over his shoulder as he demonstrates how it—whatever the "it" is that he teaches—is done, how it is lived, how one may minister out of it to others. And he will carefully watch over their shoulders as he coaches and guides them in learning the same skills and behavior.

This new teacher will be an alive, dynamic person who knows how to deal with his sin God's way, who does not hesitate to admit wrongs to students and ask their forgiveness, who grows by each experience of this sort, and knows how and when (and when not) to share his own trials and God's solutions to them with his students. He is vitally concerned about pleasing Christ, is a serious Bible student, is a prayerful person and relies on the Holy Spirit in his teaching. In short, he is dedicated to helping students grow in knowledge, life and ministry.

Much could be said to fill out this portrait in detail, but I think I have said enough to give you the flavor of things. This redeemed, self-consciously Christian, growing, changing, mature, biblically oriented teacher will be a winner. And, because he will be, the new education will spread rapidly among zealous Christians. He, in God's providence, is the one who will be used most to make it go. Because the new education demands high-level teachers, and because only high-level teachers will be interested in it, the new Christian education will prosper.

There is only one way that it can fail: if there are not enough persons who fit this description already in Christian education, or who have the courage to step forth. That, of course, is the unknown factor. I do not doubt that sufficient numbers shall come forth. But time alone will tell.

TEACHING IS DISCIPLING

It is time that educators took George Bernard Shaw's famous state-ment seriously: "Those who can do, those who can't teach." That was not merely a clever quip; sadly, it was the all-too-true observation of a shrewd observer. The new education, however, says *those who can do, those who can teach others how.*

Because the biblical model is discipleship, as we have seen, it is essential to recruit teachers who, in addition to talking about their subject, are willing and able to demonstrate its relevance and practicality for students by the actual use of its principles in real life situations. (I shall approach the subject of education-in-the-milieu in a later chapter; so hold on for a few moments.) The teacher who disciples is, himself, a model of what he teaches, not (like the academe that Shaw had in mind) a model only of some one talking about it.

Like Jesus Christ, who gathered 12 men around Him as disciples ("students"), he teaches them and then sends them off to teach[2] (cf. Mark 3:14). In Mark's summary statement, he says that Jesus appointed them to "be with Him." That is a significant statement; He does not say to "study with Him," but to "*be* with Him." He does not say to "*learn* from Him," but to "*be* with Him." This simple phrase is broad in scope and encompasses all the rest, but much more as well. The disciples received formal and *ad hoc* lectures; they learned from casual teaching questions and comments; they saw and heard Jesus in action in real life situations, living and ministering to others according to the principles that He taught; and they were able to ask Him questions.

This ability to *see* and *hear* teaching integrated into action, in real life situations, by one's teacher, is the missing ingredient in almost all Christian education. Yet, a physician, a carpenter and even a plumber are trained this way. Whenever such training is offered (in Evangelism Explosion or at C.C.E.F., for instance), people respond enthusiastically.

Also, a student, under supervision, must be allowed to participate in similar activities as his teacher coaches and helps him to integrate facts into living, and skills and attitudes into some phase of ministry,[3] just as Jesus gave the disciples authority to minister in His name while He was still on earth.

Ideally, any subject should be taught as painting is. First, one studies basic principles and theory (not for tests or for exercise, but for *use*). We do not abandon lecture altogether. Then, some paintings should be observed and studied in the presence of a teacher who can point out in them what a novice needs to learn. Next, the student should observe an artist at work, the former asking questions, the latter raising other questions and making observations ("Do you see how I am holding this brush? Well, . . ."). After this, the student must get his own brush into the paint and, under supervision, apply it to the canvas. He should do this under direction until he is able to make progress on his own, checking in with the teacher when he runs into problems, needs information, must learn new skills, and at those stages where his work is ready for evaluation and critique. After that, under supervision, he should progress to the

---

2. Mark says "preach." Preaching and teaching are very closely related in the New Testament. What Jesus did is, in different places, labeled preaching or teaching. His favorite designation for Himself is "Teacher."

3. All that we do in life as Christians, whether it has to do with pigs or preaching, should be done *as ministry*.

point where he learns how to teach others. As he succeeds in this, he may leave supervision behind and continue to supervise others. *That* is discipleship.

All of the elements in the previous paragraph belong to discipleship (with emphasis on some others, according to the subjects and skills taught); as you can see, this truly will take a new kind of teacher!

"And," you will say, "a new kind of school situation. I can't even imagine how you would set it up."

Well, let that wait a bit. For now, let us continue to talk about the kind of teacher it will take to get the new education off of the ground.

"OK, but where will you find him? Who has been trained this way?"

That, of course, is a big question. And I now wish to discuss it in an initial way.

THE ACQUISITION OF THE NEW TEACHER

You won't often find many teachers operating as I have been describing —not even in art, music, shop and home economics courses, which (doubtless) in *some* ways approach it. Sports coaches, perhaps, come closest! What teacher in a thousand teaches math for use in actual situations? And who demonstrates its use *in real life* while inviting his students to observe? And, who uses it for life and ministry, demonstrating how practical for the kingdom of God knowledge of the multiplication table can be? Virtually no one, that's who!

Well, then, what shall we do in selecting teachers? We shall present them with our program; we shall discuss it in depth with them; and, given the fact that they possess the basic parental and other personal characteristics already described, we shall challenge them to develop the new programs along with us.

Administrators will be wise to set up an ongoing teaching program at the school itself for consultation, discussion and planning, through which the new teacher learns to teach as a discipler and, in cooperation with the school authorities, works out in detail just how he will teach what. Of course, its genius also will be that it too is taught by the discipleship method.

"But that's a rather uncertain thing for him, isn't it? What I mean is that it's downright risky. Suppose he can't come up with what he needs?"

Good question, to which I wish to make several replies:

1. You have only *begun* to hear about the program. Ask your question again when you have finished reading the book. You may not want to.
2. If, in the selection of teachers, only those teachers are chosen who fully understand and are wholly committed to the program (with all its initial risks), who fit the qualifications already stated, and who are enthusiastic about the new education, few such impasses will occur.
3. Help will be given. But the fact that each teacher contributes much, itself, ought to be one of the greatest incentives to recruiting the kind of teacher that we want. And, of course, after the program gets well under way, older teachers in the program will disciple newer ones.
4. In those infrequent instances in which failure occurs, all involved will know that a wrong choice was made. But the very nature of the new education, with its challenges and demands, will go a long way toward screening out the wrong types of teachers at the door. Clearly the sorts who flee to the academic world because they think they could never make it outside of the academic shelter will not apply for positions in the new Christian schools.

"I see. But how does it work out? I mean, what, for instance, will a history teacher do?"

I can't answer that question yet in any depth because there are other pieces of the puzzle that first must be put into place. Instead, let me take that little patch of green and red puzzle and hook it together with a few other pieces that will put a somewhat larger patch in place for you.

First, in evaluating a prospective history teacher, I'd be interested in learning how the study of history has affected his life. Has he grown as a Christian through it? If so, how? Has he become cynical, disillusioned? If so, he's not our man. If, on the other hand, he has become a Christian realist who has no illusions about the goodness or perfectability of man, or the certainty of human progress apart from the gospel, but, like Daniel, has learned to read the signs of the times and can see God at work in history, bringing good out of evil and working out His purposes, I'd be very much interested in him. If he saw no effects of the study of history on his own life, I'd want to know why. If he had no knowledge of the biblical principles of history and of its interpretation taught in Daniel and elsewhere in the Bible, I'd be wary of him. But, it may be that such matters, when mentioned, would strike him with impact and would reveal interest. Then he might be considered further. At any rate, there would be a lot of discussion in this area.

But I would also want to know what he has *done* with the learning he has acquired. Has he memorized a lot of dates? Is he a walking history book? Is he merely in possession of facts but with no concern for ministry? Are there any facts of history that he relates to life today? Has he somehow become involved in ministry as the result of his historical study?

The basic question, then, is "How has history (or whatever) blessed you and made you a blessing to others?"[4]

If the prospective teacher's study of history can be justified by no greater concerns than earning a living or the satisfaction of his intellectual curiosity, then he is the wrong person for this program. Such a person may be interesting, but he will never be able to help students to take *more than an academic interest* in history for history's sake. I'd want teachers who are working on, or are committed to working on, the meaning of history for life and ministry to God's glory.

There are more than enough scholars already who are selfishly devoted to scholarship. If their scholarship—unlike Luther's and Calvin's—fails to reap eternal benefits for God's kingdom, it should not be emulated by students. There is nothing wrong with scholarship, but it must be scholarship that serves.

Students *will* imitate their teachers. When Jesus chose the Twelve to "be *with* Him," He did so in order that they might become *like Him:* "A disciple isn't above his teacher; but everybody who has been thoroughly trained will be like his teacher" (Luke 6:40). That is a powerful statement about teaching, possibly the most powerful ever uttered. A teacher may not recognize the fact, but students don't only *think* like their teachers, they *become* like them. That is to say, *in all areas of their lives* something is acquired from teachers. That is why teacher selection is so critical.

And, to complete the picture, listen to this: "Now when they saw the boldness of Peter and John and realized that they were uneducated laymen, they were surprised and recognized that they had been with

---

4. If it hasn't, there will be no way to *demonstrate* the use of history for life and ministry to students.

Jesus'' (Acts 4:13). Jesus chose the Twelve *to be with Him,* so that they would *become like Him,* and it was not long before others recognized that they *had!*

The truth is that imitation goes on all of the time, whether or not the teacher or the student is aware of it. John, for instance, doesn't command us to imitate; he *assumes* that we will. His concern, therefore, is whom we will imitate: "Dear friend, don't imitate evil, but imitate good. The one who does good is from God; the one who does evil hasn't seen God'' (III John 11). So, what happens in teaching ought to be thoroughly understood by Christian teachers. That means that if they are going to be models for their students, like it or not, as whole persons teaching whole persons (attitudes, values, behavior, etc.; not math and history only), let them model self-consciously and Christianly. That is what Paul did (Phil. 4:9; I Cor. 11:1).

Doubtless, What I have said in this chapter has raised all sorts of questions in your mind. So, let us patiently proceed, chapter after chapter, taking up each item in its place until we have enough pieces of the puzzle together for you to finish it on your own. By this time, I'd say, we have the border in place and a number of patches put together here and there. Let's see, now, if we can't find some of those key treeline pieces that will sort out the sky from its reflection in the lake and help you pull your scattered groupings into place.

13

TEACHING IN THE MILIEU

What I have said thus far presupposes quite a different teaching situation than the one we are now accustomed to in the school classroom. I have spoken about teachers demonstrating to students what they have been talking about by *doing* in addition to talking, about students *ministering* to others what they have learned (as an integral part of their learning), etc. What is in view here?

What is in view is an important principle of biblical education to which I shall devote this chapter and, in one way or another, much of what follows in the rest of the book. That principle is that teaching must occur not only in formal teaching contexts,[1] but *also in the milieu to which the teaching appertains*. But in this chapter we must examine the principle itself.

In the Book of Deuteronomy, God, through Moses, set forth a way of life for His people. In chapters 6 and 11 (especially) He deals with how parents (and especially fathers—I shall not stop to comment on the importance of male teachers in Christian education) must teach their children that way of life down through the generations.

The fundamental passages are these:

> "Here, then, you have these commandments, statutes and ordinances which the Lord your God directed me to teach you. They are the laws you are to observe in the land to which you are crossing over to possess it; so you may revere the Lord your God by practicing all His statutes and His commandments which He lays upon you, on you and your son and on your grandson, all the days of your life; and your days shall be prolonged. So be attentive, Israel; be careful to practice them, that it may be well with you, and that you may be greatly increased in a land flowing with milk and honey, as the Lord, the God of your fathers, promised you.

> "Hear, O Israel, the Lord our God is one Lord, and you shall love the Lord your God with all your heart, with all your soul, and with all

---

1. The problem in the present situation becomes most apparent when one reflects that schooling, as we know it, is entirely formal. Another way to put it is that all of the life situations to which teaching appertains must be formalized as *teaching* situations.

your strength. These words with which I am now charging you shall be written on your heart; and you shall impress them deeply upon your children; you shall talk of them when you are sitting at home, while you walk on the road, when you lie down, and when you get up; you shall bind them as a token on your hands, wear them on your forehead as a badge, and write them on the doorposts of your houses and on your gates'' (Deut. 6:1-9, Berkeley).

''When, in time to come, your son asks you, 'What is the meaning of these decrees, these laws and ordinances which the Lord our God has enjoined upon you?' thus shall you answer your son: 'We were slaves to Pharaoh in Egypt, but the Lord rescued us from there by a strong hand. Before our eyes the Lord worked by portents and marvels, great and terrible, against Pharaoh and against his whole household, against all Egypt; and the Lord brought us out from there and ensured to us an entrance here, giving us this land which He had promised on oath to our fathers. So it was that the Lord commanded us to keep all these laws and to show reverence for the Lord our God, for our welfare so He might keep us alive as we are kept alive today. This will make for our righteousness, provided we take care before the Lord our God to obey all His requirements as He has ordered us to do' '' (Deut. 6:20-25, Berkeley).

''Store up these words of mine in your heart and in your soul. Bind them as a token on your hands, and let them be as a forehead band between your eyes. Teach them to your children, talking about them when sitting at home and when walking on the road, when you lie down and when you get up. Inscribe them on the door posts of your houses and on your gates . . .'' (Deut. 11:18-20, Berkeley).

The words of Deuteronomy 6:7ff. and 11:19f. constitute a divine command to teach. There was an *imperative* for teaching children. What God said could not be kept to one's self; it must be passed on down the generations. Thus this teaching was not optional; it was required. The parental teaching of the lambs in God's flock is not an arbitrary, casual, take-it-or-leave-it activity; it is vital and important. It is done in fulfillment of a divine command.

Secondly, we see that God is concerned not only that it be done, but also about *how* it is done. For this he gives explicit directions. We shall develop that fact in detail presently.

Thirdly, the fundamental condition for teaching God's truth is parental love for God (Deut. 6:4, 5) and parental knowledge and modeling of God's commandments (Deut. 6:6, 17, 18; 11:18). Then, as it is suggested in 6:20, children will be led to ask the right questions. When the Word of

102

God is in the teacher's heart (his inner life; as the vital element in his thinking and decision-making), his outer life will have substance as backing. Commandments *"on* the heart," does not refer to memorizing Scripture portions, but to the biblical governing of the inner life, from which all thought and behavior stems.

So, in order to teach children, one must take up the task as a divine commission and must know experientially what that teaching is in his own life. Now, let us turn to the second point in more detail: God's expressed concern about *how* this teaching is to be done.

If teaching methodology had not been of importance, God would have left us to develop our own ways and means, as He does in fulfilling numerous commands. But He did not. He expressly spelled out, in detail, how he wanted this teaching to be carried on. In those directions two factors protrude:

1. The teaching is to be "deeply impressed" upon children (Deut. 6:7).
2. The way in which this impression is to be made is by teaching in the milieu to which the teaching appertains (Deut. 6:7b-9; 11:19, 20).

The word translated "impress deeply" in the Berkeley version is a single Hebrew verb that means to "say something twice" (it is related to the number two). Then, it comes to mean to "say it again," or "repeat." It is used of sharpening a sword because in the whetting process the blade is *repeatedly* struck by or rubbed against the honing stone. Every educator *must* recognize that repetition is a vital part of education. But the second factor in the word moves away from the idea of repetition as merely rote learning, to the idea of applying truth to situation after situation to which it corresponds. Surely, one must learn the truth, but repeatedly he must be shown its application to everyday, real life circumstances. Truth must be integrated with life.

Exactly what does it mean to teach "when sitting at home, while you walk on the road, when you lie down and when you get up?" (Deut. 6:7b; 11:19). And, what is the idea in binding God's Word "as a token on your hands," wearing it "on your forehead as a badge" and writing it "on the door posts of your houses and on your gates"? (Deut. 6:8, 9; cf. 11:18, 20).

Talking about God's commandments when sitting at home, while walking along the road, when lying down and when you get up means doing it *everywhere*—in all sorts of places and in every kind of circumstance. This teaching must go on at home and away from home; it must apply to all of life, at night or during the day. There is no life situation to which God's commandments may not be applied. We must teach children that all of life is under God and must become sacred to them. We must teach them that God's Word is all-embracing; there is no neutral ground in all of life; it is to be lived for Him in its entirety. That is why God requires teaching in the milieu of life.

And, in addition to this, the child must be shown by the teacher *how* to apply these commandments in all sorts of life situations. That is why parents must talk not only *about* every and any circumstance, but *in* it (when sitting, while walking, etc.). Such teaching relates God and the child to one another and to the milieu; it is teaching that takes place *in* the milieu.

Binding the commandments on the hands, wearing them on the forehead and writing them on the doorposts and the city gates again means that the commandments of God are to govern all of our behavior (hands) and thought (forehead). And this is true whether we are in our own home or city (doorposts), or whether we leave it through the city gates and go elsewhere. In all places, the commandments of God apply to every and all circumstances. To teach *that* is the teacher's main duty.

That is why the academic model is insufficient. That is why parental-like, discipling teachers, rather than academes, are the ones to be sought and secured. That is the world view in which God wants children raised.

A classroom is not sufficient for these things. Surely God's Word relates to classrooms. But it is much broader in scope than that. And lecture *about* circumstances is not the same as walking, sitting, and teaching in them.

If you see clearly how essential it is to teach children God's way,[2] and how vital it is for you to obey Him in doing so, how can you go on subjecting children to a yoke that isn't easy and light? And how can you go on furthering the modern disobedience of Christianity as you fail to heed the directives for teaching that God has given? Having discovered

---

2. We don't need sociological or psychological studies on learning theory to tell us how to teach children and how they learn best. God has settled this matter for us in the Book of Deuteronomy.

God's way of teaching children, can you go on as you have been without multiplying disobedience yourself?

"But how is it possible to break out of the classroom and to begin to teach in the milieu?"[3] One way to do so is the subject of the next chapter.

3. If, after reading this book, you are convinced of its soundness and of the imperative for change, you may find yourself faced with a dilemma. You may discover that you can find no one who appreciates these matters. In such cases, I suggest that you begin to talk to administrators, parents and other teachers about them. Ask if you and another teacher, together with a select group of students whose parents are enthusiastic about doing so, may run a pilot program for several years to allow the option for those who want it, to demonstrate its feasibility and, in time, to provide a program for comparison with the academic model.

14

MINISTERING PROJECTS

BY-PRODUCTS

The program that I shall outline in this chapter (*only* outline) will provide a way for the Christian teacher to break out of the classroom into the milieu of life. Not only will this effort provide opportunity for a greater obedience to God in making teaching of the sort that He commanded possible, but, as always, the inevitable result of obedience to Him will be many incidental blessings.

One such incidental, but important factor, will be the breaking up of the present monolithic peer society to which our children are subjected, which has done so much harm. Their friends, to which they turn for advice, guidance, and support, are peers who are as confused and as messed up as they. The adults, whose guidance and help they ought to be seeking and so desperately need, are missing in the necessarily professionalistic atmosphere of the academic situation in which the teacher, with his tests and grades, is pitted against the student rather than becoming a trusted friend, a coach, a companion, and a confidant. Breaking the academic hammerlock on the school will free teachers to stand *next* to students (as a football coach does) rather than *over against* them.

In conjunction with this, there will be a natural teaming up of teachers with students, as together they confront the world, instead of the present teaming up of peers against teachers. It is unbelievable, but sadly true, that in Christian schools (all the way from elementary schools through theological seminaries) we find this student-versus-teacher stance, which humanism has brought into being. Consideration of this serious problem alone ought to make it obvious that there is a mandate for radical change in Christian education.

Secondly, there will be a trend away from the current tendency of so many students to become academic bums, always taking school, hanging around colleges and universities when instead they ought to be out in life contributing something. Many of these students, with good minds but with a fear of going out into the rain, try to remain under the protection of the academic roof as long as they can. Then, when finally forced by finances, etc., to leave, they do not know what to do with their lives. Many of them end up on the trash heap.

Early instruction and experience in integrating truth with life, accompanying teachers who take students along and teach them out in the highways and byways of life, and who in their own lives exhibit this integration, will go a long way toward dispelling that fear. When one has been taught from the earliest days, both by precept and by example, how to integrate truth into life and ministry, he will be largely prevented from becoming an academic bum. He should, instead, look forward to moving out into the world to undertake on his own those occupying and controlling tasks that for years he has been learning in that milieu. The school—public and Christian—has been a misused hothouse, ill-equipping students for life in the world as it really is.

And, lastly (though many more valuable by-products might be mentioned), teaching in the milieu makes the school (and its teachers and students) a blessing, and its program a ministry to the community. The school that I envision is not a selfish society, shut up within its own four walls for most of the day, doing its own thing. Rather, it will be a dynamic force for good, not only for the students (schools have lost sight of the principle that it is more blessed to give than to receive, and students are forced into the role of receivers only), but for the community at large. Part of the refreshment of Christian education is found in the blessings that are received from giving.

Well, so much for the positive side-benefits of teaching in the milieu. Here, I wish to observe that such teaching is the biblical method for teaching children that was mandated by God. As a result, it will have good results in "deeply impressing" truth on them, and there will be many beneficial educational spinoffs from this. But how shall we do it? Practically speaking, how may one go about getting a school into the milieu of life while teaching? It is clear that Jesus took the disciples around with Him while He did his work. But, in our modern situation, how can we best approximate what He did?

MINISTERING PROJECTS

Fundamentally, there are two elements that must enter into any proposal for teaching in the milieu:
1. In one way or another (there are various options here), teachers must

be involved in projects in the community, or in projects that can be related to the community. These must be projects that provide for them a growing experience and enable them to use their teaching specialties for Christ in ministry to others. Moreover, these projects must provide opportunity for students to observe what they must learn through what their teachers are doing.

2. Likewise, there must be projects of all sorts for students as well. These may be the same or projects similar to those in which their teachers are engaged. Projects may be carried on in homes, in churches, out in the community, or at the school for some such segment of the community.

PROJECTS RATHER THAN COURSES

There is opportunity for much variety in details, and for many differing approaches to the solution, but the one factor that must remain constant in the program is the substitution of projects for courses. These projects may already exist; in such cases, students and teachers may simply plug into them. In most cases, perhaps it is better (for purposes of control) to become involved in projects conceived, fostered, and/or sponsored by the school, or by churches, individuals, the city, businesses, and other institutions *for* the school, according to the school's requirement.

These projects, ministries, project ministries, or whatever you may prefer to call them (I have no brief for the word), as I said, will take the place of courses. They will be *real* projects in the sense that each one, whether on-going (like running a printing service for the Bible-believing churches in town) or one-shot (like writing and publishing a book for use in other Christian schools, or scripting and performing a play), will have a genuine in-the-milieu, for-the-milieu objective (or series of objectives). Services will be advertised, money will be spent, commitments will be made and kept, responsibilities will be met, and a satisfactory job must be done. These projects are *not* to be conceived of as exercises or tests, but as *genuine tasks in which actual ministry is carried on.*

A project differs from a course in a number of ways. First, a course focuses on one aspect of life (logic, history, grammar) *to the exclusion of other aspects;* it exists in isolation. A good project, on the other hand, is well rounded (as life-in-the-milieu itself is) and emphasizes many aspects of life *at once.*

Secondly, a course teaches theory in the abstract, without application to real life. There is little more at stake than grades. Even when a lab is required, though the lab may add a dimension, efforts expended are still nothing more than exercises; there is no element of commitment or ministry bound up with them. The principle of learning for use in ministry is totally lacking. Even the lab course is selfish and focuses on the student alone.

The successful completion of a project integrates all of the elements of real life. Let me mention a few of the numerous studies that must be made, let us say, to produce an original play:

1. Theory must be learned for every aspect of writing, directing, advertising, producing, and promoting the play, but (*please* note), theory is learned *for*—for writing, directing, etc.—in short, for *use*.
2. Skills must be developed and used. A play will involve historical, grammatical research, the ability to do woodworking and painting in order to construct first-class scenery and other props, the mathematical and other matters relating to lighting and sound must be studied, etc.
3. Ministry must be accomplished (the actual production of the play that was written for churches, old folks' homes, etc., is the goal). Along the way, interpersonal relations among staff and cast will be a matter of concern.

These and many other such matters will afford learning/living/loving opportunities for students and teachers alike.

"But how would all the information and skills necessary for a child to learn in 12 years of school be taught through projects?"

Answer: much more thoroughly, more interestingly, and more lastingly. *Everything* now taught in courses (plus more) could be taught through projects. The differences would be that in the project learning the student learns for doing (achieving the goals of the project), in life situations (integrating facts into living and skills) and in order to bless others (using data and skills for unselfish purposes). And he learns on several fronts at once. What a difference!

The new education will mean the development of a brand new curriculum, from the ground up, built around multiple projects (several often running concurrently). These projects will be designed and sequenced in such a way that *in order to complete them*, certain desired segments of data and skills will be required—the very ones thought necessary to learn over a student's 12 years of study. Of course, the 12-year period could be up for grabs too as it is reviewed. It may be found, as I suspect, that students will mature and will progress much more rapidly in the project program, and that might lead to a number of adjustments. A year or two of what is now called general, background college work also might be undertaken during that period.

In time, projects by the scores might be designed. These would include alternate projects for each stage in learning, from which some would be selected in any given year to meet current needs and opportunities, to avail one's self of the resources providentially provided at any given time among parents, teachers, and other interested segments of the community, and to meet the strengths or weaknesses of any particular group of students.[1]

But, secondly, in response to your question let me ask one or two: "Is the material that schools now teach (or attempt to teach) all worthwhile? Is all of it necessary for all students? Is not much that is valuable for life missing? Are there not many more important matters than learning a long list of historical dates?[2] If, in order to complete a given project, it were necessary to learn lists (of anything), they would easily be learned—as easily as data on baseball players, teams, etc., that students want to learn to use. But we must ask fundamental questions about what *is* and what is *not* necessary. This matter I cannot discuss in a book as general as the one you are reading. What is important to say here is that the *entire* body of factual knowledge now taught must be thoroughly reconsidered, and judgments about the value and place of such information must be made. Omissions in present curricula must be noted. Nothing must be taken for granted.

These projects will go a long way toward sorting out gifts among students and putting them on the right tracks for life. Over the years, a student will have opportunity to try out various sorts of life activities and, presently, will gravitate in a certain direction. Coming up to the twelfth year he will not *begin* to ask, "What has God gifted me to do in life?" In the pursuit of his place in projects, he will have been faced with that

---

1. Records of every project, with details, should be kept by each school and published (a project in itself) for other schools to use. Soon the selection will take place from among a wealth of possibilities.

2. Who, for instance, is to say that ability to identify the principal flora and fauna in one's local community would not be more valuable?

matter throughout and by then should have a very good idea about what to do.

Projects will stimulate much more thorough learning. And, at long last, everyone will know, not from uncertain tests and grades, but from actual performance and from the feedback coming from those who were recipients of the project's ministry, how well a student learned in it. In this program, one *must* learn; the achievement of the project *depends* on his learning. If one is performing poorly, something will be done about it. He will be helped (in a coaching manner), shifted to a different aspect of the project better fitting his gifts, counseled about personal problems that hinder, etc. And, as I shall mention later, learning for doing will more highly motivate learning. And, finally, note: one learns more quickly when he has to produce.

If projects replace courses, school buildings will change shape. There will be classrooms, where theory is taught and seminars are held, but not so many of them. There will be other rooms that look more like workshops. And there will be a larger warehouse or storage area for project materials. Garages, or almost any other sort of structure, may have to be built (as a project, of course). The buildings will be an ever-changing beehive of activity. But learning will not all take place on school property; the property is the *hub* or base of the school—its campus is the entire community.

Many individual and community resources will be used *on location*—shops in basements of parents' homes, the offices of a local business, etc. So, it will not be necessary to do everything in one building.

Students will find it necessary to go and come frequently to discuss matters with local suppliers (here teachers or parents can supply rides), to negotiate with them, make purchases, etc. In this way again the peer-only context of education will be shattered.

Let's say that a high-school-age group that has successfully completed a number of projects surveys the Christian schools in the U.S. and Canada to determine what needs there are among them to which they might minister. (This itself is a good project, involving research, statistical and marketing skills, and leads to another project. And notice, by this time, under supervision, the students themselves are designing projects!) Among the many responses they receive (some of these may be handed over to teachers working with different groups or filed for succeeding classes) is the need for a textbook on the basics of botany written from a

111

Christian perspective. The group is anxious to write, print, and publish it. This is an ambitious undertaking. It will involve a large investment of time, effort, and money. And it will run some risks. The group will be required to run feasibility studies. These studies may show the group that it would be biting off more than it could chew. Even so, the experience of considering and abandoning the project and the feasibility studies would themselves be valuable. But suppose, among other things, the studies showed:

(1) a high degree of feasibility;
(2) the project probably will involve X amount of commitment for Y amount of time leading to Z results;
(3) the project will be marketable if ACSI or a Christian school publisher can be encouraged to publish and distribute it;
(4) a local printing company will train two students in the use of its equipment and will allow the book to be printed at cost if these students, in exchange for the skills learned and the use of the equipment, will each give 50 hours of free labor to the printing company during the next year (of course, they would be learning still more about the printing business during this time);
(5) etc.

Already, you can begin to see something of the many areas of facts and the numerous skills that must be mastered to achieve the goals of the project. There would be research, writing and editing skills, photographic and layout design theory and skills (all to be learned, along with the mathematical understanding necessary), the mechanical skills of building, plumbing, and wiring a darkroom, printing and binding skills, and more. Knowledge and skills not possessed by teachers would have to be (1) learned and/or (2) found in other places (e.g., the printing company).

And, consider how varying gifts of different students would be uncovered, challenged, and developed. There would be true diversity in unity. In order to be sure that all would learn something about everything, progress seminars would be held periodically. At these seminars, the ''experts'' in each area (the students deeply involved in it) would be required to report on what they are doing, explain how and why they are doing it, and respond to questions and observations from the whole class and from teachers. At times, they would even lecture briefly on what they have learned. Problem-solving sessions also may be held, in which the whole project group discusses various difficulties as they arise. In these ways, everyone would learn something about everything; each would learn much about some things.

For various reasons (sickness, moving, etc.) usually more than one person will work on each area. Students will work in teams of two or three within each group. And, where it is possible to do so on a given project, for wider exposure, teams may even be switched from one area to another. And, as one phase of a project is completed, various teams (or members of teams) will find it possible to be reassigned. Plenty of variety and flexibility should be built into the larger project designs.

And, at last, through projects we will get truly integrative team teaching! Efforts at team teaching have largely failed. And the reason is that it doesn't work in an academic setting. It has failed because academic teaching *requires* no team. Academic education fractures life artificially and fights against an integrative approach. There can be little team effort by specialists who are merely talking theory. But put specialists together *on a project,* and you will get team effort *par excellence*—just as you do during an operation, when anesthesiologists, surgeons, nurses, and other technicians team up, each lending the benefits of his specialty to the total effort to get the job done. It takes team *work* to make teamwork work!

Will teachers be specialists? Yes, but not specialists isolated in a "department" located in an ivory tower. (All departmental structures will be pulled down.) They will *use* their specialties in projects, and they will learn (*mirable dictu!*) in true team teaching that theirs isn't the only specialty that counts! Teachers, like students, will learn from their colleagues. And teachers, like students, will receive the blessings that come from participation in genuine ministry. There aren't many blessings in exercises and tests!

"But will there be no exercises and tests? How will the students learn skills?" There will have to be simulations, of course. There will be first efforts. But as in an aerospace project, these all will be closely related to project goals—to the ministry to be accomplished. And projects will be given in proper sequence: proceeding from simple and more basic ones to the more complex and more refined. That means that a high-school-age group producing an original full-length play will previously have done all sorts of similar, but more elementary, projects (producing original skits for lesser ministries successfully prior to taking on this more ambitious assignment). Their work in elementary school and junior high school[3] projects will prepare them for high school projects.

Much, much more could (must) be said about projects, or school ministries (especially in the area of curriculum), but that is the subject of another book, or series of books, yet to be written. All I can do here is to sketch out the outlines of the program. But this outline, rough though it may be, I believe offers enough detail for anyone who wishes to do so to understand, catch the vision, and run toward it. It will be filled out a bit more in the chapters that follow.

---

3. There must be rough grading according to age (labels like elementary school and high school *may* be retained if it is understood that these are not rigid categories, but bench marks) and according to one's level of achievement and completion. This grading will have more to do with his performance and his growth, however, than with his age. Certain projects (e.g., a play) will allow students of various ages and performance levels to be thrown together at points. Such mixing, if not overdone and if carefully monitored, will be encouraged.

15

UPGRADING BY DEGRADING

I have written about knowledge, life, and ministry as goals for Christian education, and how these may be integraded in the milieu in controlling and occupying projects (or ministries). Projects replace courses, ministering replaces "taking subjects." But what of evaluation? How will evaluation be done?

Not by grades!

MacArthur said, on his forced retirement from the army, "Old soldiers never die; they just fade away." At the time, a number of parodies on that statement were made, one of the best of which was, "Old teachers never die; they just grade away." It is interesting that grading was selected as an outstanding characteristic of a teacher today. Surely there is good reason for this.

As I approach that sacred cow, therefore, I am sure that I shall raise as much ire and as many eyebrows over what I have to say, as I shall about the entire program itself.

Grading is a modern, 100-or-so-year-old innovation in education.[1] It was not always with us. Most of the world's greatest thinkers grew up in an educational system that knew nothing of grading. Yet nothing I know of has caused more problems and more trouble in schools than grading. Grading causes problems for parents, for children, for administrators, for teachers—for everyone. Still people tenaciously hold on to it.

Here we must examine grading in the light of biblical principle. We have merely accepted grading unthinkingly, without asking questions. We simply took it over from the public schools.

GRADES AND GIFTS

God has gifted all Christians: "Now there are different kinds of gifts, but they come from the same spirit, and there are different kinds of service, but they are for the same Lord, and there are different kinds of results, but the same God accomplishes everything in everyone" (I Cor.

---

1. Kirschenbaum, Simon and Napier, *Wad-Ja-Get?* (New York: Hart Publishing Co., 1971), p. 51.

115

12:4-6). Gifts are just that—gifts. They are not earned. And they come in a wide variety of sizes and shapes, distributed "separately to each one as He [the Holy Spirit] determines." These dispensations of gifts are not subject to the whims of men; differing gifts are the result of the sovereign bestowal of the Spirit. Gifts differ in kind, in purpose, in results, and in measure. The picture is that God gives different Christians different gifts for different immediate purposes, but the long range goal is benefit for the whole kingdom.[2]

Since God gives different gifts, and even the same gifts in different measure, why should we expect to fit everyone into a comparative grading system? When we do this, are we grading students, or are we grading the Holy Spirit? What we need to do is to discover individual capacities and encourage individuals to develop and deploy these to the full. It is totally wrong to unfavorably compare one child's intellectual ability with another's and to grade one above another because of his abundance or lack of ability in the same area.

Paul sketches a picture of unity in diversity (I Cor. 12:26). The eye needs the nose, and the nose needs the ear. All are important. Prep schools that exclude students not so well endowed intellectually should be anathema in Christian education. The message of such prep schools is that, in spite of all that Paul says, eggheads can do very well without the farm hands or the flat feet on the beat. But verse 22 calls these seemingly "weaker" members of the body indispensable.

And the school is a part of the body of Christ. Children come with differing gifts, largely undeveloped, many undiscovered. It is the school's task to enable students to discover, develop, and deploy their gifts. It is not the task of the school to grade them. Why do we favor those who possess the more intellectual sorts of gifts over those with the more manual sorts of gifts? That, in effect, is what academic grading does.

When we grade highly those with the more academic gifts and fail those who may be faithful Christians, but gifted in other ways, we have judged God. These children whom we fail and cast by the wayside may be cheerful and useful in their homes and might be fine helpers in the

---

2. Some may argue that these gifts do not involve abilities that make a difference educationally. But *every* gift of the Spirit (both extraordinary and ordinary), when considered carefully, in one way or another is closely related to learning ability. Since persons are whole persons, it could not be otherwise. Some gifts (e.g., teaching, ruling) require large intellectual capability; others (e.g., helping) may require far less.

church, contributing much to society and God's kingdom, but, during the 12 most formative years of their lives, our schools repeatedly send them the message that they are no good. And for 12 years they and their parents are miserable. Is that the way for Christians to evaluate one another?

There is no way that this comparative, competitive system can be justified biblically. We do not look around the congregation Sunday morning and say, ''O, there's an A student, there's a C,'' and so forth. You don't and shouldn't think of people that way. God doesn't teach us to do so, and He doesn't speak of His people like that either. But through modern school practices that's how we teach our children to think about one another and themselves. We evaluate people (or should) on a much different and much broader base.

Typically, there are children who are a pleasure at home all summer long, but who, from October or November on (when they irretrievably fall behind in their academic work), become a blight on the home and in the class. They are nervous, irritable, miserable, confused, and angry. The school system—with its academic grading messages—has provoked them to wrath (cf. Eph. 6:4). No wonder so many parents and children sweat out years and years of such behavior, only to end with strained relations toward their children or with children becoming runaways or dropouts from society!

Those daily, grading (or should I say, degrading) messages—''you're no good!''—year in and year out, make it difficult for sinful children and parents to survive. When I see increasing numbers of children from Christian homes in trouble, I am not so much disturbed over those homes (which, for the most part, have done all they can, unavailingly), but about the Christian schools that, in large measure, have provided occasions for such a deplorable state of affairs. I think that the problem is most acute in Christian schools, where the emphasis on ''high academic standards'' has been increasing; the pagan school down the street may have given up in despair over ever achieving such excellence. No wonder castoffs from Christian schools often ''do better'' (i.e., get higher grades, or at least somewhat less grief for child and parents) than in the Christian schools.

This grading mania, which has captured American education during this century, was unknown during the thousands of years of educational history preceding. It was begun, not for the benefit of the student, but for

117

the convenience of colleges.

Unless we grade all of a student's life, from making beds to playing football, we should grade no single segment of it. To deify the intellect above everything else in life is humanistic idolatry. And its effect is to make second-class citizens out of those with lesser intellectual endowments. Worse still, Christian prep schools disenfranchise them altogether! God hasn't; how dare we do so? The biblical doctrine of gifts precludes it altogether.

Writing numbers (or letters) on paper, next to some child's name, is potentially among the most dangerous and damaging crimes that can be perpetrated against him. And yet, in spite of all contrary evidence, because of the virtually universal acceptance of this practice, most parents and teachers think that grading is not only essential, but good. Before I am done, I hope to show you that it is neither.

If there are differing gifts (Rom. 12:6), there must be varied offerings in Christian education, designed to discover and develop all of them. A uniform, academic curriculum does not do that; the project program will. The uniform academic program demands conformity, and, by grades, it penalizes those who refuse to be troweled off into uniformity, either because they won't be leveled into something that God didn't design for them or because they simply cannot. The project approach nurtures and exalts the differences God has made; the academic grading approach ignores differences and tries to treat everyone alike; in doing so, it smooths out important variations and specialty-orientations and tends to bring about mediocrity. Grades are the visible expression, by the narrow-minded, insular academes who have captured American education, of their intolerance of persons whose interests and abilities are dissimilar to their own.

Even if you look at the general genetic differences between boys and girls, you are confronted with distinctions great enough to demand separate programs. Boys learn with emphasis on the right hemisphere of the brain; girls with emphasis on the left. The right hemisphere is concerned with the non-verbal and with learning by manipulating the environment. The left hemisphere focuses on learning by listening.[3] Why do you suppose that ninety percent of the children labeled "hyperactive" in our elementary schools are boys? When you realize that in the

3. Richard Reitak, *The Brain, the Last Frontier* (New York: Doubleday & Co., 1979).

early days academic training tries to fit boys into a mold that only forms much later, but that comes naturally for little girls, the statistic shouldn't be startling. How far behind we are! We don't even make *that* sort of distinction in education, let alone the further sorts of distinctions that stem from differing gifts.

Only God's curriculum—teaching knowledge for use in life and ministry, in the milieu—can meet all the demands. We didn't need to wait for information about hemisphere emphasis in learning to do the right thing. That was all considered by the One who designed the human brain and told us how best to reach it in childhood.

The project approach is one way of implementing those biblical principles. No other program that I know about appears to take them seriously. No other curriculum avoids leveling and mediocrity, which are part and parcel of the academic/grading approach. The project/ministry approach offers opportunity for *all* to excel in something.

GRADES AND GOALS

Now, let's look at another matter. Grades discourage worthy goal-setting, and, in particular, those goals that are essential for every Christian student if he is to use the gifts of the Spirit in relation to the fruit of the Spirit (you can't grade love, joy, peace, etc.!).

Grading encourages students to work for grades rather than for other goals. They work to get good grades, not to please Christ. Students no longer work for understanding useful knowledge and skills; they don't do school work to become better persons, and less and less to be able to serve Him well in later life. Students are becoming caught up in grades and in their importance (above all else) for getting ahead in life. They work no longer for goals but for grades; grades have become the goal of modern education.

One reason why so many college student do not know what major to declare is that they have no goal except grades. All their lives they have worked for grades, and now they are "just taking college," working there also, as before, for grades. This situation has been growing worse. "High grades so I can get into the college of my choice" is the sort of thing you hear. Life, meaning, purpose, and ministry are all but completely by-passed in this frantic push for grades.

Grade-oriented students learn to study teachers instead of content: "How can I give each teacher what he wants to get a good grade? Will this teacher want me to put the emphasis on detail or cover a broad sweep generally? Does he want his own words back, or does he want me to contribute my own thought?'' These are the sorts of concerns to which grading gives rise. Kids are learning to ''psych out teachers,'' as they put it, not their course subject matter. They learn content *only for the sake of grades,* and *only so much as is necessary* for getting good grades. Then they retain content *only long enough* to get those grades. Our children are being cheated out of an education by the pursuit of grades.

''But don't grades motivate? Isn't it necessary to motivate students by grades?'' Grades motivate all right; but in the wrong ways, for wrong ends. They motivate students to cram, to con, and to cheat.

GRADES AND GOODNESS

Grades are potentially dangerous numbers or letters for another reason. They become a stumbling block for many students. Paul, in II Corinthians 6:3, warns us against placing stumbling blocks in anyone's way. But this warning is particularly true in regard to children. Note well Christ's strong language in Luke 17:1, 2: ''Then He said to His disciples, 'Stumbling blocks are sure to come, but woe to the one through whom they come! It would be better for him if a millstone were hung around his neck and he were thrown into the sea than that he should be the occasion for one of these little ones to stumble.' '' It is a serious matter to do anything that would cause problems for children; especially problems that might hinder them from coming to Christ. How many children are being turned off from Christianity by its ''high academic standards,'' which are so clearly manifested in grading? How many children have been tempted to cheat because of these standards? The matter is not a casual one; it has serious implications for all concerned. If grades are a stumbling block[4] that puts strong temptation in the way of many (perhaps the majority) of our children, as I believe a careful study of the matter will make clear, then we must do away with them.

Grades encourage cheating. Listen to this report in *U.S. News & World Report:*

At the University of Arizona, a student manipulates the school's computer, raising the grades on his transcript.

At a Boston university, a premed student pours a caustic acid into the

---

4. A ''stumbling-block'' is an unnecessary and humanly induced temptation to sin.

laboratory flask of a rival, destroying data that took months to accumulate.

A senior at the University of Colorado, shortly before graduation, offers a professor $200 in return for an A grade.[5]

And why is this cheating becoming such a problem? Read on:

"Students know how extremely important it is to get top grades to get top salaries," asserts Ron Blatchley, director of student affairs at Texas A&M University. "Money in the bank is the bottom line."

Randy Herbertson, student-body president at Colorado, says cutthroat competition for grades spurs desperate actions by students. "You can walk into any chemistry lab and cut the tension with a knife," he says.

And while you're at it, don't miss this:

Educators agree that the jockeying for spots in graduate schools of medicine, business, law and engineering has created a junglelike attitude on campus, with students competing with each other for straight-A grades. For some premed students, a B in a key course can be catastrophic.[6]

Grades, grades, grades! That's what you hear in this article. They *are* a stumbling block. Grades motivate all right; they motivate students to cheat. Grades encourage cheating, apple-polishing, and the sacrifice of integrity in order to pander to teachers so that they will give better grades.

Teachers and educators who have studied the problem know that grades are unreliable, unfair, invalid, and rarely significant—and they often have trouble with their own consciences.[7] Over 50 different criteria for grading have been distinguished, and the possible number of combinations of these used by given teachers is enormous.[8]

As a teacher at the University of Missouri and at Westminster Theological Seminary, I often wondered about grading. I knew how subjective it was; a lot depended on how I felt, what mood I was in, etc. Often I

5. Note, especially, the words "rival" and "competitive atmosphere."
6. Oct. 20, 1980, pp. 39, 42.
7. Studies for a long time have shown that teachers do not grade alike, and after an interval of time teachers do not grade the same papers in the same way. Kirschenbaum, et al., chap. 12. The spread of grades in science and math, not just in English and history, was A-F for the same papers handed to different teachers.
8. This study, ibid., and most of this information on grading, has been available for over seventy years. Clearly, grades are retained for reasons other than to benefit students.

gave higher grades just because I knew I couldn't trust my own judgment when not feeling up to par. I know the struggles of conscience that a teacher can have over grades, and talks with other teachers have made it clear that I am not alone in this matter.

"Objective" grading does not exist. The selection of questions, wording of questions, type of questions used are all subjective factors. Then add a sprinkling of the 50-odd criteria for grading, and who knows *what* you will come up with? Grades reflect the personality and the attitude of the teacher and the student at the time as much as they do anything else. Don't kid yourself into thinking your grades are objective; every study shows that they aren't. If you are self-deceived about this, that is all the worse. In any case, therefore because grades lie in what they say, they are immoral. Because they are immoral, they lead to immoral thought and action on the part of those tested.

Moreover, grades support bad teaching. Teachers, who have no other hold on students, continue teaching year after year even though their teaching is abominable, and are able to maintain their positions only because they can manipulate parents and children by grades. Before the advent of the grading system, the *teacher* also was evaluated. People asked, "Did the student produce under him?" If students had been required to show competence as the result of a teacher's work, these poor teachers would have been dismissed long ago. What it boils down to is that they maintain their jobs by force; and grades are the weapon that they use.

And speaking of force, grades create forced *competition* between students. Go back and reread the quotations from *U.S. News & World Report*, and you will become aware that the fierce competition I am speaking about is the underlying theme. Friendly, voluntary competition of various sorts is one thing, but *forced* competition is quite another. The word "percentile" is an intrinsically competitive term. Grades set friends against one another and—what in many ways is worse—against teachers. Note the word "rival" in the *U.S. News & World Report* article. Is that what Christian schools should do—encourage rivalry?

Galatians 6:3, 4 is pertinent: "If somebody thinks that he is something when he is nothing, he deceives himself. But let each one test his own work; then he will have something to boast about in himself alone, rather than comparing himself with another." This passage makes it plain that God wants none of us comparing himself with another. What we ought to do is evaluate our *own* lives, against the standard of our own potential and our obligations before God. Paul *forbids* competitive evaluation.

"But doesn't God grade?"

No. He judges by performance. He says, "by their fruit [i.e., what they produce] you will know them" (Matt. 7:20). He tells us that the final judgment will be on the basis of works (Matt. 25:31-46; Rev. 20:12, 13.).[9]

And, it must also be remembered, God offers grace and forgiveness to his erring children. Where is forgiveness in the legalistic grading system? There is no place for wiping the slate clean and starting afresh. Repentance and forgiveness are unknown concepts to humanistic grading systems. There is nothing but hard, cold, unrelenting, degrading grades.

"But we grade work, not people." Wrong. It is the *people* who did the work who are being graded; try to tell *them* that it is only their work! How can the work that one does be separated from him? As Christ said, the fruit tells us about the *tree*. We may be grateful that God is more merciful in Christ than most academic professors.

THE WAY OUT

Grading has shut us up in a box; how can we break out? The way out is by degrading the system rather than the students. All of the halfway compromises won't work; the only thing to do is to eliminate grades altogether.

But, then, will there be no evaluation? Of course there will: "by their fruits you will know them"; we shall evaluate by performance and competence. There are a number of ways of doing this. If you retain the idea of credit, it could be granted for so many achievements. Better still, the right to move on to the next project may be conditioned on successful completion of a project that is prerequisite to it.[10] And, why can't we encourage and help each student along the way to see that he *does* make it? In project-learning teachers have much more time for individual help. Teachers are coaches, who should work to produce a winning team for Christ.[11]

---

9. God saves by grace through faith alone; but He says that judgment (the separation of the one from the other) is based on fruit (works): the tree (whether one is saved or unsaved) is *known and judged* by its fruit (what it produces: works). Cf. *More than Redemption*, p. 301.

10. In case of sickness, inability, or unsuccessful effort, special individual projects may be used.

11. The one teacher who most approximates the biblical teacher is the coach. He doesn't give grades, he helps the student to learn, encourages him to do so, teaches him

Proficiency is what we want, not grades. Studies have shown that grades tell very little about one's proficiency or capability. And they certainly don't tell anything about the student's spiritual growth (one of the major goals of truly Christian education). Then, too, how do you grade ministry? The laughable grades in practical theology in seminaries make that clear enough.

Already, colleges are ready to accept those who are from ungraded high schools.[12] They evaluate students on the basis of interview, portfolios of work, tapes of speeches, letters of recommendation, and tests. Indeed, students coming this way often get special attention and have the opportunity to say *more* about their work than those who merely send transcripts of grades.[13] Just about all college admissions committees know that grades alone mean very little.

So, I challenge you to think hard about grades. After doing so, you may grade this chapter F, but that won't bother me a bit (you see, I don't believe in grading). Actually, the grade you give it probably tells me as much about *you* as anything! Seriously, will you not reconsider the whole question of grades—for the sake of your students and the honor of Christ?

MAKING THE GRADE WITH STUDENTS

When you fully abandon grading, you will discover (as I have) that you can develop an entirely different relationship with students and with their parents, one that will go a long way toward making teaching a truly refreshing experience. Now, you and they *together* can struggle side-by-side to solve problems rather than expending your energies in counterproductive struggles with one another. Eliminating grades is the greatest single factor I can think of for terminating the teacher/student adversary relationship.

One final point: teacher, let me remind you that when you lay aside grading you relieve yourself of one of the most foolish, futile, time-consuming, heart-rending chores in modern teaching—one that is entirely unnecessary and unrewarding.

---

for use (in real sports events), and—above all—does *not* sustain an adversary position. The two work *together* to overcome a *common* opponent. All teaching should be like that.

12. Kirschenbaum, et al., pp. 70ff.

13. A senior project for each student might be to compile a portfolio with a resumé of high school achievements, etc., for presentation to a college or a prospective employer.

16

LEARNING FOR DOING

"But if you lay grades aside as an option, how do you motivate children?"

That is an important question. When God required children to be discipled in the milieu and for life and ministry, He knew what He was doing. A part of what He was doing was to set forth the most vital motivational program of education ever. Of course, as sinners, we have ignored it—to our own hurt, and especially to the detriment of children.

Note three strong motivating factors in the biblical program:

1. Teachers discipling students by their example, as well as by precept, *demonstrate* the importance of, feasibility of, and methods of using what they teach. Working side-by-side with students, they build encouraging relationships.

2. Teaching in the milieu makes classroom talk (theory and exercise) come alive. Demonstration on location helps integrate truth with reality.

3. Teaching for doing gives purpose, meaning, and perspective to learning, especially when the doing is in the context of ministry to others.

Now, *there* is a motivational program with a kick!

Just consider, for a moment, a student under the present system who is wrapped up in the production of his class yearbook; to the consternation of the academes, he'll devote more time to that work than to homework.[1] Or take the student who becomes a prop man for the annual school play—again, you see the same thing! Why? What *motivates* him? Real interest, coupled with the sense of satisfaction that grows out of achieving something worthwhile. It is amazing how much time and energy is expended on such projects (note what they are)—and not for grades!

---

1. Incidentally, in our program all homework must cease. Child/family relations are already strained too far for anything else to separate them as homework so effectively does. Families ought to be able to do things together at night, unhampered. Homework assignments, for the most part, are exercises and one of the clearest admissions that the schools don't teach. Enough "natural" homework, unassigned, will occur when students are motivated through projects.

These students are *learning for doing*. They will study all sorts of matters, do extensive, detailed research (or whatever it takes) to achieve the real-life objectives (the play *will be given;* the yearbook *will be published*) that they have in view. On the other hand, you may find it difficult to get these same students to do homework exercises three out of five nights in a week. Another student, who will not study math for exercises or tests, *will* study (and learn) all the technological intricacies (even mathematical ones) connected with a motorbike that he wants to properly maintain. These students are motivated to learn because they are *learning for doing*. They know that their learning will be put to use. And they know that unless they learn what is necessary for it, they will not be able to achieve their real-life goals.

For Christians, learning for doing takes on a still larger dimension that Christ called "refreshment" (see previous chapters). Jesus spoke of this not only in Matthew 11, but also in John 4:32, where He said, "I have food to eat that you don't know anything about." He spoke of an inner satisfaction that comes from doing God's work, which was as heartening as the satisfied feeling one gets from eating a good meal. Ministry to others, in which God is given His full weight, learning for doing *good,* is like that. It is "blessed" to "give" of one's self. In contrast, learning for selfish ends alone brings the opposite results. Learning in the institutionalized programs that we now support is nearly all receiving; no wonder it is hard to motivate the student! Such learning for tests, for exercises is, in the end, learning for grades. But grades have no truly refreshing, or even satisfying effects because of the self-centered purposes in view. When one learns to live and learns to love, he learns in ways that are beneficial and satisfying to him *as a by-product,* but, of course, if he learns in order to be satisfied, he will *not* be. Satisfaction and refreshment, like happiness, peace, and joy, must never be sought. The *pursuit* of these things is always in vain. Rather, they come unexpectedly when one selflessly seeks to honor God and the welfare of his neighbor in what he is doing. Learning for selfish ends is not edifying. One grows only as he learns *in order to give*.

Learning to use correct grammar isn't the same thing as learning how to write stories or plays. Satisfaction comes from the latter, little from the former (unless it is seen as a means of doing the latter: learning grammar for use). But, beyond that, learning to write stories *as a ministry* to young children, or plays for actual evangelistic uses on the beach, is *refreshing*.

126

Learning takes place when one knows that what he must study is essential to accomplishing what he wants to achieve. Contrary to what many educators think, they have not served a student well when they have motivated him to learn for learning's sake. When he begins to do that he has begun to set up learning, the intellect, etc., as idols to be worshiped, and when that happens, you can be sure that he has been thoroughly contaminated by the academic system itself.

Because no one learns for exercises, students who do learn well, and do complete exercises well under the present system, are those who have learned to add their own "for use" goals ("If I learn to do these exercises well, I shall be able to . . ."). This goal may be good grades, to do better than Mary, to win approval at home, or to maintain an average high enough to play on the football team. But whatever it is, more likely than not, the goal (when not coupled with a giving, ministering view) will be a goal that is inadequate before God.[2] Motivation comes from the prospect of producing; and the highest form of such motivation comes from knowing that what one is producing pleases God. Take away grade-motivation, and at last you will leave room for confronting, challenging, and persuading students to work for this higher motivation.

"High school is an alienating experience for many young people [and] like a prison." That is what the Carnegie Counsel on Policy Studies in Higher Education concluded three years ago.[3] No wonder, when you consider the low motivational package that institutionalized education has to offer!

Math and language ought never be taught as "subjects"; to do so destroys motivation. They should be related to such projects as high-level photography, using a computer, writing books, or making speeches—all, of course, for use in ministry. They are tools—means that are used in reaching ends. How to use a camera or make a speech should not be related merely to getting a better job, or acquiring a hobby, but, in some way, to serving Christ.

Motivation occurs on several levels. Motivation at the outset and along the way also can differ. A husband leaves home. It isn't wrong for his wife to want her husband to return, but it *is* wrong for her to try to get him back "at any cost," as she puts it. Her first motive must be to please

_____

2. Paul says that self-serving learning blinds one to the truth (II Tim. 3:7), a dimension of the problem to which I do not want to address myself here.

3. Macon *Telegraph*, Nov. 28, 1979.

God in the crisis, *whether her husband returns or not*. Otherwise, she'll do what God says as a gimmick and stop if her husband does not return. So there is a *priority* in motivational counseling goals. The same is true in education. A student (or group of students) determines to write a play for the benefit of the old folks in the nursing homes where it will be given. But, if that is the *only* motive in view, or if it is the *highest* motive in view, the motivation is humanistic, man-centered. The play must also be done to honor God. And that top priority motivation will (1) condition all that is done in its production as well as (2) bring a different result to all concerned. All sorts of plays could be written merely to amuse or cheer them, if uplifting old folks is the only goal. But one will be sure that he uplifts with *biblical truth* when his motive is to honor God. The two do not compete when the priorities are right. All good, but subordinate, motives are in harmony with the greatest one. But they turn humanistic when they stand alone or are sought above the glory of God. Lesser goals must be viewed as *means* to attain greater ones.

Motivation is important in education because there is so much to learn and it must be learned over a long period of time. Unless motivation is maintained, and growing, it soon can be lost. No wonder, then, that by the time an improperly motivated student reaches high school, school has become a "prison" for him. This can happen easily for students who are motivated only to seek selfish ends. Indeed, some of the more highly moral students are the ones most seriously affected. They know that life ought to consist of more than selfishness. But school offers them nothing else. To have schooling that is a pleasure (the best condition for learning), a child must be motivated by the cause that refreshes. This refreshment, growing out of labor profitable for Christ, strengthens the student and encourages him to carry on. High school is the time for challenge and commitment to ministry; it is a time of idealism and hope. What a shame to turn off and "alienate" young people! This is the time to truly motivate. *Ministering projects* (or project ministries, if you will) of greater challenge, complexity, and benefits will do just that.

Sameness, though it has its place in terms of framework and basic principles, dulls motivation when all pervasive. The academic model reeks of sameness. Projects, in real-life situations, with all of their built-in variety and unknown contingencies, are like life—full of surprises. This fact helps to sustain motivation.

The fact, too, that much hangs on the outcome of the project (more than a grade or completed exercise), and that this has to do with God and others rather than merely one's self, is important to motivation. The results of projects affect life and have eternal consequences (sometimes large ones). How a student acts in a play may have something to do with the sanctification of members of the audience and the cast, as well as his own.

Moreover, peer pressure becomes a positive force in ministering projects. If there are deadlines to be met, and everyone is meeting them except the photographers, the other members of the group will put strong pressure on the photographers to do so (so strong that, at times, a teacher may have to moderate it). Incidentally, the ways in which such problems are handled is a part of education. Important principles of biblical problem-solving and interpersonal relationships learned in such real-life contexts are invaluable. And, in project ministries, not only will there be time to address such matters; the success or failure of the project may hang on whether or not one does so.

I have mentioned teachers discipling students, demonstrating, supervising, helping, and working alongside of them in projects; this very scenario is highly motivational. Such close, loving, encouraging, and enthusiastic concern in teaching is of the very essence of motivation. What will motivate a 3-year-old child to jump off a diving board into the deep end of a pool the very first day of swimming lessons? I'll tell you what *did*—a "Y" teacher who with excitement and laughter jumped off hand-in-hand with my daughter. She loved it, now swims like a fish, and even teaches swimming, life saving, and water safety herself. That is the result of discipling motivation.

The same will be true of students. How can you get a 14-year-old out into the world of business, dickering pleasantly and successfully with an adult supplier about the price and delivery date of 50 reams of sulphite bond? I'll tell you: by a teacher or parent taking him along on similar trips and showing him the ropes. What will fire up a group to write and perform an evangelistic skit on a nearby beach better than watching a group of teachers do it first?[4]

---

4. By the way, teacher, doesn't this sound like a much more exciting and profitable type of teaching than grading exercise papers? If you respond yes, immediately, you're probably our sort of person; if no, you may not be. If the no stems only from fear of such freewheeling discipleship, then perhaps all you need is some motivational discipling yourself.

As you can see, motivation is multifaceted. But, to mention one more source, the teacher's own enthusiasm, and enthusiastic participation in learning for new projects and new ministry may be as important as any other secondary motivation. Such a desire to learn can be contagious. A teacher with a vital faith will not only communicate it to students, but will find that such teaching procedures will enable him to grow as well. As present, institutionalized, academic structures cramp all such enthusiasm and its expression; teachers become bogged down in academic detail, never minister, and fail to grow. No wonder students and teachers alike dry up under such artificial, sterile, and spirit-smothering conditions.

17

A WORD TO ADMINISTRATORS

There are many things that could be said about the work of administration. You may find that it will depend on you to get the new Christian education off the ground. You may discover it would be exciting for you, and for some students with administrative gifts, to do some administrative projects from time to time, in which you (1) get student assistance (not the major motive) while you (2) give them a taste of what it is all about. But, while I could go on suggesting areas of this sort almost indefinitely, instead I shall focus on a few points in outline form (for ready reference):

1. You will select teachers. When you do, keep the following in mind (see also, chapter 12):
   a. A teacher should have parental characteristics (why not write out a list of these?).
   b. He should be an enthusiastic discipler whose Christian life and ministry could be imitated with profit.
   c. He should be a serious Bible student (ask him about his favorite commentaries, Bible dictionary, what concordance he uses, his evaluation of the NASB Bible, etc.); you'll learn quite a bit about his Bible study practices by doing so.
   d. He should understand the new education and be sold on it.
   e. He should be flexible and creative and anxious to contribute something fresh to his teaching.
   f. He should know his specialty area well.
   g. He should be able to demonstrate how his specialty has blessed his life and how he has used it in ministering to others. This is of special importance.
2. You should stand behind your teachers and encourage them.
   a. Let them know where they stand with you at all times; never keep them in doubt.
   b. Encourage them (cf. II Cor. 8:22, 23) as co-workers.
   c. Help them to work with parents and to work out all differences that arise. Teach them to face difficulties rather than to avoid them.

d. Do not be too ready to take sides; be sure of facts. Require evidence from parents who bring accusations against teachers. Hearsay is inadequate.
3. Help your teachers as their servant, while, at the same time, exerting *proper* authority. Keep the two in proper biblical balance.
   a. Provide help promptly when requested or needed.
   b. Provide training in the new education.
   c. Provide time for Bible study for application to teaching and resource books for it.
   d. Provide know-how on project design and integration of truth into life and ministry.
   e. Support all truly biblical innovation.
   f. Provide help in personal trouble. It is better to invest time in preserving a teacher through counseling than to lose the years of investment in him (study *Ready to Restore* and other biblical counseling books for help).
   g. Provide a yearly biblical counseling training program for your teachers.[1]
4. Keep communication flowing.
   a. Deal with problems promptly.
   b. Teach, and practice, confession and forgiveness. Don't dismiss teachers for doing wrong, but for failure to repent and change.
   c. When necessary, call on church discipline. The school isn't the church and cannot usurp its work.
   d. Make communication direct, personal, frequent, timely. Don't let intermediaries distort messages.
5. Learn to delegate.
   a. Delegate jobs; never do anything a teacher, parent, secretary, or student can be taught to do as well or better.
   b. Delegate authority to do the job.
   c. Learn to trust individuals, and then to hold them responsible.
   d. Delegate jobs to *individuals* with the gifts and enthusiasm to do them, not to committees.
6. Remove as much red tape and paper work as possible.
   a. Cut out all that isn't *absolutely* necessary.

---

1. A videotape series, complete with workbooks and in color, is available for such purposes. For details, write C.C.E.F., 1790 E. Willow Grove Ave., Laverock, PA 19118.

b. Look for new, less demanding ways to accomplish the same ends.
c. Be wary of teachers who like paper work. Are they really concerned about children?
d. Free up teachers for *teaching* as much as possible.
e. Use parents freely for as many chore-type jobs as you can to free teachers for teaching.

If you do these six things faithfully, you will facilitate the work of Christian education through a happy family of teachers and staff and an effective program.

18

EFFECTING THE CHANGE

Feasibility; that's the bugaboo that, even in the case of those who are otherwise sold, will stand in the way. It always does.

Is it possible to make the change? Is the financial side feasible? Is it realistic to think about dislodging the old order? Are there not too many persons with vested interests? Can all of the many obstacles be removed? Is the change but a pipe dream? Is it idealism run wild? Wait a minute—those are the wrong questions.

If the change *ought* to be made, it *can* be made. If it is *right* to make the change, we *must* do so—even if we can't see the feasibility at the outset. The right question is, "Is the change biblical—does God *want* it?" If it would honor God to make the change and greatly benefit our children, then we *shall* remove the obstacles. If God requires it, He will make the way. God never requires anything of His children that it is impossible for them to do—*His* way, in *His* strength. So the *real* question is not whether or not it is feasible, but "Is it biblical?" If you say yes to the latter, then you *must* say yes to the former.

Convinced, as I am, that the program is biblical, and therefore feasible, I am more concerned about *how* best to effect the change in a proper Christian manner than any other issue. Here, in doing the right thing wrongly, more trouble can be stirred up and more bad press for the program can result than, perhaps, from any other single factor. So let's go back to the blackboard and consider the matter.

There are several problems to solve:

1. *The proper authorities must be persuaded.* Teachers, parents, administrators, and boards all must be persuaded, *not necessarily of the rightness of the new education* (though that would be ideal), but at least the rightness of giving an opportunity to demonstrate its superiority and rightness. If you can get that far, you will have gone a long way. Most persons will not be persuaded by a book or by argument alone. If, in your situation, they are—so much the better. In most cases, you will have to *demonstrate* what you have been advocating.

2. *A detailed pilot program might be proposed.* Do not expect those who are not enthusiastic to do the work for you. You will have to develop a pilot program on your own. When you have it ready, propose it, in detail, as a pilot program to be pursued by you and a few others to test and to demonstrate the new education.

3. *Allow enough time to iron out the wrinkles.* Make at least a five-year proposal. You will need time to develop it, to sell and enlist a small enthusiastic core of parents and teachers to participate, to face and solve many unforeseen problems, for students to adjust, for the program to get under way and to begin to make impact. In some cases, seven years might be a better length of time.

4. *Enlist enthusiastic participants only.* You don't want skeptical, unenthusiastic, or opposing parties participating as teachers, students, or parents. All persons involved ought to be screened carefully by careful consultation with them. They should understand thoroughly what you have in mind. Parents and teachers probably should have read this book. You do not want teachers who will sabotage your effort, purposely or by apathy, students who really don't care one way or another, or parents who will criticize failures. Doubtless there will be a number of false starts. Everyone must recognize this and be able to live with it. Indeed, what you want is hopeful people who want to see this effort succeed so much that they will do everything legitimate to assure that it does. They should pray regularly for it. They should rally to solve problems. They should be ready to give time. Don't start until you have a group like this; if you start too soon, with uncommitted persons, you may set back the program indefinitely.

5. *Sell the program more widely by demonstrating it.* Most people won't believe the bumblebee can fly if shown the specs on it. But they believe when they see it in the air! The same will be true of any new proposal. Don't become disgusted with persons of little faith. Thomas was blessed for believing after having seen. Thomas remained a disciple even with his show-me approach.

6. *Make no more claims than that you are trying to be more biblical.* If what you do doesn't pan out, lay that not to a failure on God's part, but to a failure somewhere along the line on the part of men.

What I have written above is advice for making a transition from an institutionalized program to the new education. But in one way or another most of what I have said applies to freshly starting a school from scratch. Go slowly, work with people; don't try to sell with talk alone; ask for an opportunity to demonstrate. We believe in projects, not merely the academic approach. We know, therefore, that we must *disciple* people into new ways.

Remember, change comes hard. Many people like things the way they are. Others don't like things as they are but fear change might lead to something worse. Be patient, loving, winsome, and firm. Respect persons with honest differences, but refute their errors. Consider what you are doing itself a project and use all the principles of motivation that you have learned. Be a discipler for the new Christian education.

There is no magic formula for effecting change. Mostly it is a matter of persuasion and demonstration. When some programs get under way, it will be possible to arrange visits to see the new education in action.

But there are some who will not change. After considerable unsuccessful effort, over a reasonable period of time, it may be necessary for you to look elsewhere for another situation. For a while, you may find it hard to locate a suitable one. With your convictions about the new education, and about the changes that must take place in order to effect it, it is only honest and honorable to inform any prospective employing institution of your beliefs. You should accept a position only on the understanding that you will work (in a proper, Christian manner) toward eventual change. Express your interest in a pilot demonstration program rather than total change at the outset. You will find that even a pilot program is too radical a proposal for some schools. Later on, when a number of schools begin converting to the new education, it will be easier to convince such schools of the desirability of giving it a try.

Because of your convictions, you may find yourself out of a teaching job for a time. You should be aware of this possibility and count the cost.

A DIFFERENT SORT OF SITUATION

Should a conservative, Bible-believing pastor, administrator, or board happen to gain control of a school that, though boasting the name "Christian," doesn't possess even the minimal accouterments of Christian education, a school in which the very salvation of the headmaster and most of the teachers is in doubt, in which evolution is taught in the biology classroom, abortion is taught as an acceptable option in psychology class, etc., then there is only one thing to do. At the cost of much bloodshed and agony, with which he should fully reckon before proceeding, he must place a bomb under the whole thing, including both personnel and program. Pilot programs will not work. The whole sad enterprise must come down at once, and a brand new start, from stem to stern, must be made from whatever assets remain. Situations like this cannot be changed in stages, piecemeal.

In bulldozing the existing school under, it is only right to give fair notice well in advance to both parents and personnel. A clear-cut declaration of purpose (I almost said "of war"), together with a reasonable timetable, a statement of faith, and a detailed outline of the new curriculum and methodology for implementing it, should be supplied to all concerned. Explicit job descriptions for teachers and other staff, including individual interviews, should be made available to all of those in the present program who think that they could meet the new requirements. You might be surprised to find one or two Christian teachers come to life who, with proper help and encouragement, would fit.

At any rate, radical change like this may cost the school its community reputation (which will have to be rebuilt on a better basis), students, funds, and other sorts of backing. On the other hand, if carefully managed, with everything done lovingly and aboveboard, the move should gain approval and support from the genuinely Christian community.

All misunderstandings and/or matters involving gossip, bitterness, hostility, and so on, that usually accompany a change of this nature, should be dealt with promptly and straightforwardly, in a distinctively Christian manner. There must be much prayer throughout the transition.

THE UPSHOT OF IT ALL

Change in institutions rarely comes easily. Is it feasible? Yes. Will it be easy? No. You are probably in for trouble if you determine to see your school transformed. Prepare for it; courageously work for it. Pray for it. And, as you win the opportunity, demonstrate it—convincingly.

19

MISCELLANEOUS MATTERS

Before concluding, I want to consider a remaining hodgepodge of miscellaneous matters important enough to receive mention, though not at such length as to require a full chapter for each.

1. **Some other things that every student should learn at school:**

   a. How to serve God.
   b. How to evaluate all matters according to biblical standards.
   c. How to use the Bible in everyday affairs.
   d. How to discover one's life calling.
   e. How to choose and acquire a life partner.
   f. How to live and work well with others.
   g. How to make decisions and solve problems God's way.
   h. How to raise children.
   i. How to work in the world as a Christian.
   j. How to live at home as a Christian.
   k. How to care for and properly use the body.
   l. How to do research.
   m. How to control God's creation.
   n. How to relate to people God's way.
   o. How to develop and use occupying (social) skills.

2. **Should there be a Bible course?**

Yes and no. That equivocal reply means, first, that the usual sort of Bible course—one that teaches Bible content alone—is not needed. Often such a course is cosmetic, the "proof" that a school is "Christian." It duplicates material taught in Sunday school and church. *Everything* that is taught in a Christian school should be taught biblically, from a biblical perspective.

Secondly, the *use* of the Bible is to be taught by showing students the practical use of the Scriptures. Christians need to learn how to use the Bible to solve problems that arise in the course of ordinary life activities. This sort of teaching should be done throughout, but with special emphasis for those of junior high age, who are beginning to solve problems. A book, *What to Do on Thursday,* which could be used for help in this matter, is now available.

3. Discipline

I have ignored discipline because the same biblical principles of discipline that must be used in the home must also be used at school. A study of these may be found in my book, *Christian Living in the Home.*

4. Authority

There must be an authority structure in the school. Again, the structure is the same as in the home. Students must be taught to honor and obey teachers as they are required to honor their parents (Eph. 6:1-4). But, as in the home, it should be clear that the teacher, as well as his student, is under Christ's authority, and that all valid authority exercised is, in the final analysis, His.

5. Play and games

For very small children, play seems to be what work and study is for older ones. Through play and games they may learn skills, facts, interpersonal relationships. Teachers must use play for teaching purposes.

Athletics and other sorts of games will need to be given special consideration in another book. One thing is for sure, many of the cheers and much of the basic "We're #1, trounce the bums!" mentality that we hear have no place in the repertoire of a Christian school.

6. Financial feasibility

It is possible for the school (or for groups of students) to form corporations (profit or non-profit—there are options) for various projects and enterprises that (a) would provide projects and (b) would return revenue to the school. Money, however, must always be a subsidiary factor (a by-product). First is ministry, second, personal growth; then, somewhere down the line after these, funds.

If the I.R.S. ever removes the tax exempt status from Christian schools, the new education, since it is based on projects that produce, will be in an excellent position to sustain itself better than the exclusively tuition/gift supported schools. Projects that are not financially responsible will not be undertaken. Part of every new project will be a feasibility study. In mathematical *exercises,* in present academic circles, students can play around with millions of dollars; but they are only playing Monopoly. But in a project, where success or failure may depend on feasibility, students learn to balance Christian realism with vision and faith. Certain projects, good in every other way, will be scrapped because not yet feasible.

7. Commitment from parents

The new school will require more of parents; consequently, they will get more out of it. Precisely what a school requires (there is room for much diversity here) should be spelled out in detail, in writing, and it should be understood and agreed upon by all parties. School and parents should contract for these obligations prior to the opening of school.

8. Hardware

Various technological teaching devices are now available to schools (video tape, computers, etc.). One of the problems with purchase of these has been lack of use. Academic programs do not encourage such use. Discipling for real living does. However, no equipment should be purchased unless there are people available who can teach its use and maintain it, and unless it truly aids projects. Project design, on the other hand, should take into consideration all present hardware and attempt, wherever possible, to utilize it.

9. Some suggested projects (just a few starters)

a. Write and produce skits, plays, musicals for evangelistic purposes, use in churches, old folks homes, etc.
b. Run a printing service.
c. Build something—a garage for a poor widow, a boat for the school's marine life explorations, etc.
d. Run a tax service.
e. Publish a weekly Christian newspaper.
f. Run a repair and fix-it shop.
g. For little children: map out the route for a field trip. Figure out the time, distance, and expenses required. Make arrangements with the bus company, etc.
h. Run a catering service for churches.
i. Do a survey for a church, trying to determine where to locate.

j. Cooperate with local businesses or companies in doing a community project.

k. Help catalog the local library—advise on books to remove, obtain.

l. Find ways of helping out in local government.

m. Build and run a museum.

n. To learn typing, run a college typing service.

o. Develop a Christian think-tank for use by churches.

p. Develop a local TV program, possibly giving Christian commentary on the weekly news. [1]

q. Start a Christian grocery co-op for families in the school.

r. Video programs could be produced for use in churches, other Christian schools, etc.

s. Build a greenhouse and grow plants for botanical studies, to sell, to beautify the school, etc.

t. Invent new Christian teaching games; market and sell them.

u. Set up and utilize a recording studio, a video set or two, etc. Make cassette tape series for other schools, etc.

v. Run a research service for college students.

w. Develop an illustration clipping service for local pastors.

x. Do an archeological dig.

y. Set up a photography studio and lab.

z. Design a project designing process.

10. At length, after a school is running well, it may wish to consider its ministry to other schools. Such a school might run annual training sessions for teachers and administrators, whom it will disciple on location.

---

1. The first small project done every day at school, by the way, is to distribute the daily paper(s) and digest and analyze the news. A half-hour discussion, from a Christian viewpoint, summarizing the analysis on audio tape might be done. These tapes, dated and filed, could be used as the basis for such a weekly program. Letters regularly should be written to people in the news, to the editorial page of local newspapers, etc.

20

CONCLUSION

WHERE IS HERE?

We have come a long way. Much has been said; I know much more could be (needs to be) said. But too much for a first thrust would do more harm than good.

Many questions yet remain to be answered. There are answers to all of them. All the answers to all of the questions may not yet have been found, but they are there to be found. How do I know that? I know it because I know that God requires nothing of His children that is impossible.

The title of chapter 5 is ''Where Do We Go from Here?'' The answer to that question must come first. But the answer differs, of course, depending on where ''here'' is for you. If you are already convinced and anxious to move ahead, then go back and reread chapter 18. In it you will find your answer. If, on the other hand, you are enticed by what you have read, but are not sure, ask some of your friends to read this book. Then gather them together and discuss the matter.

If you are a teacher or administrator who is intrigued, but you wonder if you could ever convince your school constituency, talk here and there (not divisively) to various members who, you think, might be interested and find out. If you are a parent who wants this education for your children, then distribute copies of this book among members of the board, faculty, and administrators. Get other parents to read it too.

If you are very dubious, hostile, or even apathetic about what I have written, so be it. Perhaps in time, when you see it working, you will change your mind; perhaps not. I ask of you one favor: represent my view fairly when you argue against it. For instance, don't go around saying, ''He's going to destroy any real learning children now do—they won't even learn the multiplication table.'' They will, and much more, even more thoroughly because they will learn it all *for doing*.

Where do we go from here? We go forward. It is time for an advance in education. We have seen no basic change for a long time. And some of the few innovations we have adopted (grades, for example, Dewey's learning by doing) really have been setbacks.

It is time to correct the course of Christian education. We must not go on mimicking the ways of humanistic education. In this book I have sent you back to the blackboard to do your sums again. The old ways do not add up; they are contrary to the Bible. I have helped you to see the possibilities of education in a biblical mode. Now it is your turn. If you have learned anything here, you have learned that you must turn truth into action. There is something *you* can do today to bring about the change of which I have been writing. Decide what it is and get to work!

APPENDIX

DESIGN FOR A THEOLOGICAL SEMINARY*

Today it is almost axiomatic for laymen and pastors alike (less frequently, this is even heard among theological educators) to criticize theological seminaries for the inferior product that they turn out—and there is good reason for doing so. There have been far too many poor preachers, inept counselors, mediocre leaders, etc., pouring forth from the halls of our seminaries. Many of you who read these words know how frightfully ill-equipped you were when you graduated. No wonder there are so many wrecks along the way—lives of would-be ministers, shattered on the doorsteps of first or second pastorates, and congregations split three different ways! Clearly, it is time for a change! By making your concern known to your alma mater or your denominational school, you—as a pastor—can make an impact that (perhaps, in time) will bring about the needed change. That is why, in the sketch that follows, I have suggested some concepts you may wish to explore with those seminary officials upon whom you might have some influence.

How shall the change be effected? Where shall we begin? Shall we bulldoze everything in sight; shall we merely make a few additions to and alterations of the status quo? Neither approach will do. What is needed is radical, basic change, largely within the present framework (loosened up to accommodate it). The suggested proposal that follows has a number of points that cover the whole territory, but it holds together as a complete program. The details must be left to those who actually effect it.

VISION

Those who found a seminary, or who radically change its course, must be men of vision. They cannot think narrowly or negatively. If they do not see clearly where to go, they should not begin the journey. Far too often, evangelicals have shown a great lack of vision.

---

*Reprinted from *Journal of Pastoral Practice* 3, 2 (1979).

Vision in goals and programs (to be discussed later) is absolutely necessary. But, here I first mention one thing of lesser importance, though not unessential. Because it is concrete, it often shows the way the wind is blowing, the sort of support one is likely to receive, and the commitment (or lack of it) that a board actually has. I am thinking of the sort of property, building program, and provisions made for the seminary and its programs. Boards must not think merely of the present (or even near future); they must be far-reaching in their outlook.

A seminary needs an expansive outlook. Not only ought it to expect to train future leaders of Christ's church, but a seminary with a truly adequate program will attract many men already pastoring churches for a large variety of continuing education programs. There will be many opportunities for instructing laymen—especially elders and deacons. Conferences of various sorts will be held. The seminary grounds will provide the physical location for any number of special meetings; indeed, a seminary—for the sake of the students and faculty as well as others—ought to be a constant beehive of Christian activity, study, and thought, a focal (and rallying) point for Christian programs. Grounds and facilities designed for such purposes ought to be conceived from the outset of any new concern for seminary education. If such events are worth taking place—if it is proper to give time and thought to them—the seminary should promote them and thereby bring its students into contact with them—right on its own grounds. A vital mix of classroom and ministry must be maintained at all times. Not only will bringing pastors back onto the campus for continuing education and sprinkling them freely into classes with undergraduates help to achieve this mix, but also providing a large variety of meetings and activities such as I have just described.

Students must be challenged continually with the application of truth to life and ministry. Otherwise, they will tend to become cold, bookish, academic, boring in their approach to God's Word. *Above all else,* everything possible must be done to avoid this, while encouraging a warm, vital, life-changing, committed outlook instead. Cramped thinking—coupled with dusty study—accounts for much of the failure of modern seminary education. Vision—even in the design and purpose of seminary facilities—can do much to offset such dangers (more basic solutions to the problem follow). Narrow, stingy thinking about the physical plant is a clear indication of a board's lack of vision.

PROGRAM

Over the years, conventional seminary training has exhibited both excellencies and failures (so far I have spoken only of the latter—let me here emphasize the fact that there are many good things that *must not* be abandoned). While retaining (for instance) the high level of scholarship that most seminaries seek to achieve, and the clear doctrinal stance that one associates with a seminary to which he adheres doctrinally, changes must be made. It is a mistake to think that the alteration of method and goal in a program designed to bring about a better finished product must necessarily weaken scholarship or doctrinal emphasis. It may, of course, but if the program consists of a more fruitful outworking of what that scholarship has unfolded and what that doctrine points to (and now yearns for), changes for ill need not be feared. Mostly, objections to change come from (1) those who see an unbiblical disjunction between scholarship/doctrine and life/ministry, or (2) perhaps more frequently, those stodgy professors who don't care to be unsettled from their comfortable perches in theological halls, where they can chirp endlessly about the most esoteric aspects of biblical study which happen to interest them, but which provide little help for budding young pastors who will probably never use such "truth" in their ministry. This happens when professors, themselves, become detached from the ministry of the Word. The model of a seminary (and seminary program) that follows deals summarily with this problem.

How shall we begin to improve upon the program that we have at present, radically changing it, while retaining its excellencies?

First, I propose to *add* a fourth year of training, plus three years of update and advice, and new goals, together with a fresh approach to teaching and curriculum.

I expect to explain these proposals in sequence. N.B., however, I cannot spell out all the details—these would (necessarily) differ from place to place anyway. Indeed, a proper sort of faculty, gathered together with the leadership, should enjoy doing just that. Right now, then, I can offer but a *sketch*.

FOURTH YEAR

The first change that I suggest is a significant one. Let's comtemplate it for a time. This fourth year will not be added to the end of the present

147

three; nor will it interrupt them (as the so-called "clinical year" does). Rather—and this is the new feature—it will occur at the outset. This will be a required pre-seminary year prior to taking residential work at the seminary itself.

This year will be spent in a local church. In that pre-selected congregation the potential seminary student will follow a prescribed program designed by the seminary and supervised by pastors and elders who have been trained by the seminary to do so.

During the year, the prospective student will test his gifts, be exposed to all aspects of the pastoral ministry (including many of the problems involved in it), will be carefully evaluated by the church, will study the elements of Greek by cassette and correspondence, will do a good bit of basic reading, study English Bible, and (the hope is) will grow in many ways that will truly prepare him for the three-year seminary program.

What are some of the reasons for this pre-seminary year? Let me suggest just a few (there are many others).

One fundamental reason is to break up the academic syndrome found in so many students, whereby they find it possible to proceed from kindergarten through graduate seminary training without stepping outside a classroom into the rain. They have no practical experience whatever, know little of working with people, think of pastoral work only from a theoretical viewpoint, and don't even know how to ask practical questions.

This year is structured to screen out—and to screen *in*—students. Some, who do not belong in theological seminary (and, even theological educators will tell you there is an abundance of these), will never make it; others, who are not yet ready to be thrown immediately into the seminary context, will be better prepared as the result of spending this time in a warmer, more personalized context. These days there are many conversions taking place during college years—especially (it seems) during the senior year. These students often think they are called to the ministry, but have had no time to *test* their gifts. Some are called, some are not. Those that are not will profit from the year and be directed into another course. Those who are, but who have little acquaintance with the pastoral ministry, will gain much. Men who have been converted long before, who are quite familiar with the ministry, etc., can profit by beginning to develop skills and facing new problems in a more intensive ministry.

The acclimatization of foreign students (always a problem for the seminary as well as for the student) for a year in a congregation will be a very positive factor. They can learn about the American church scene, become better acquainted with the English language, and (in general) become assimilated into the American culture in a loving way. Interested church members can be of great benefit to them while (themselves) being blessed for their loving concern.

And, of course, that year will provide more *time* for training. Moreover, the student will come to the seminary with a notebook full of practical questions in all areas of pastoral ministry (prescribed, reviewed, and approved for admission) that he wants answered during his seminary training (before graduating from the seminary, these answers again will be reviewed and approved). His own inadequacies in ministry will be more apparent to him, as well as his strengths, so that he will be more sensitive to those areas where he needs to concentrate his efforts to acquire the requisite information and skills to become a competent minister.

But of first importance, the pre-seminary year will allow the church to tell the seminary who is fit to be trained for the ministry of the Word—rather than the other way around. For too long the shoe has been on the wrong foot. This fact will place the responsibility where it belongs—upon Christ's church. The church can better evaluate a man's gifts, attitudes, abilities, and commitment because of its peculiar context. The church, ideally, should be willing to put enough confidence in a man to elect him to an office in the congregation during that year. Ideally, only ordained men bearing the church's official approval should enter seminary.

The pre-seminary year will fit into an overall program in any number of ways—there should be flexibility built in—but one basic format looks like this:

Pre-seminary year — September to June
August   — elements of Hebrew at seminary
September on   — three years at the seminary

In this way, both the elements of Greek (done during pre-seminary year) and the elements of Hebrew will be out of the way *before* the student begins his three years of seminary training. This allows use of the languages in all courses *from the beginning,* and keeps those language courses from vying with other studies (as they so frequently do now). In the long run, better language training is possible.

Following the three years in resident seminary training, there will be three more years of updating and advice.

THREE POST-SEMINARY YEARS

What is this update and advice? And what is involved in postgraduate training? Basically two things.

During the three years following graduation, each graduate will receive two free weeks of update each year—that is, information about new facts, data, discoveries, studies by faculty members, new trends in the Christian world, etc. This will update students, but it will also tend to keep faculty members in touch with the practical concerns of pastors.

And, perhaps of greater significance, the graduate will be given personal advice on his pastoral ministry. During those first three years, more congregations are destroyed and more young pastors are lost to the ministry than at any other time. This addition will be an attempt to conserve men and preserve churches. Just think what it would have been like for you to have been able to do this, pastor!

The first three years (six weeks in all) would be tuition free to graduates (a limited number of others may come for a fee), and graduates may continue to come thereafter for a fee. This yearly two-week period of update and advice might be included in a January winterim sandwiched between two semesters. This, too, might be a good time to train pastors as supervisors for the pre-seminary year. Other activities fit this slot nicely too.

GOALS

New goals must be set for the three-year residential program at the seminary. Two dimensions must be added to the current focus of the seminary. Presently, the emphasis of the typical seminary is upon knowledge—its dissemination and acquisition. This emphasis on knowledge *must not be diminished*. Basically, all the knowledge now taught (though esoteric specialties of certain professors, overlap in courses, etc., should be eliminated) in a good seminary should be taught as it has been (though, as we shall see, in a different way). But we must not be satisfied to stop there. New goals must be set that will demand more of the seminary than it has ever offered before (but note, the new structure provides more time to do it). To the goal of imparting knowledge must be added two more—life and ministry. The student must be taught to turn knowledge into life and then into ministry; it is not enough to graduate men who are intellectually competent thinkers, they must be holy-living persons who are skilled in ministering truth to others in terms of their lives and ministries. The new, threefold emphasis of the seminary would be upon truth, growth and skills; each of these would be thought important. All three would be inseparably related. Thought would be shown to lead to living and ministry; living and ministering would be shown to depend on truth, etc. The seminary would undertake, *in all that it does,* to train students to apply truth personally and in ministry to others.

TEACHING AND CURRICULUM

Now, how are we to pursue these goals? A fresh approach to teaching and to curriculum will lay a basis for the change that will help to attain these goals.

Curriculum

First, let's take a look at curriculum. I cannot develop a full curriculum in this article; and each seminary faculty and administration will want to do this on their own anyway. It will be necessary for them to sit down and do the following:

1. Define and describe the finished product that a seminary ought to produce.

Many seminaries don't even know what sort of person they ought to be graduating. When we don't know what we are aiming at, we are teaching in the blue. Teaching in the blue can be fun, and even interesting, but we deceive ourselves if we think this is the way to develop well-trained, properly equipped ministers whose lives are exemplary. Objectives should be clear—agreed upon by all (otherwise, there will be grit in the gears). Every faculty member should not only *know* what the graduate should look like, but should know what he must contribute to that finished product and should be committed to doing so. *There is no place for dissension on this basic issue.* More concretely, the faculty should agree on the knowledge, lifestyle, and skills that a graduate should possess.

2. Define and describe the raw product that a seminary needs in order to produce that finished product.

Frankly, my impression is that many seminaries haven't the foggiest idea (apart from grade averages) about the qualities a seminary student should bring to the seminary (or how to evaluate a prospective student for them). Until this is decided, they will continue to accept unfit men who will be a grief to the seminary and to churches and who will, themselves, be miserable in the ministry. Once the seminary has defined and described the raw product in detail, it can structure the pre-seminary year to test for the requisite qualities and to develop them to a desired point prior to admission into seminary. The screening out/screening in process during that year can be the most useful feature of all for the seminary.

3. Define and develop a curriculum (and a methodology that is appropriate to it) that realistically will enable the seminary to move from that raw product to the finished product in three years.

One way to do so follows—again, only in sketchy form. Yet, it is an outworking of all that has preceded.

To begin with, stop departmentalizing the seminary. Departments tend to become little seminaries within the seminary; they are often clubs that have their own interests (rather than the total picture) in view. They tend to fracture the approach rather than integrate it. By all means, emphasize the specialties (development of peculiar gifts) of each faculty member, but minimize or (better) eliminate departments altogether.

In place of the departmental emphasis, structure the curriculum around the functions of ministry. In this structure, all the valuable knowledge currently taught would still be taught—but not as the province of each department. Rather, there will be a new slant, a new stance in the teaching. All will be given an avowedly pastoral and ministerial focus. Everything taught now should continue to be taught, not as part of separate disciplines, but from the stance of life and ministry. Hebrew, for instance, will not be an academic discipline; it will be a way of understanding God's Word for one's own personal growth and in order to bless God's people. *All* that is taught must have the three goals (knowledge, life, ministry) in view at all times. Teachers must teach, not in order to train other teachers, but to prepare men for ministry.

First, then, the faculty and administration (perhaps in conjunction with a number of key pastors and laymen) must define the functions of a minister of the Word (I can't do that here). Then, on this new curriculum structure, each faculty member brings his special perspectives to each function. This will tend to keep the focus on the *reasons* for teaching any given course. Those reasons will be based not on what the catalog says, or on how many hours a man ought to teach, etc., but on what a student needs for ministry. Thus, with these objectives clear about each function, both faculty member and student alike will be more likely to study with ministry on their minds.

Here is *one* way that this might be done. Let us say that we should divide pastoral functions into four broad areas of missions (including evangelism, home missions, foreign missions, etc.), edification (including preaching, teaching, Christian education, fellowship, etc.), administration, and worship (four broad areas in which a pastor ministers to his congregation[1]). And, let us say, these would form the *basis* for the curriculum (that is, [1] everything taught would contribute to one or more of these areas; [2] everything would be taught *with a view to contributing* to them). Then, sections (and/or subsections) of each area would constitute distinct teaching units (or courses). Each section and subsection would be considered from the historical, exegetical, theological, apologetic, and practical perspectives of various faculty members in terms of knowledge, life, and ministry. There would tend to be more team teaching than now—but of a sort calculated to enhance rather than inhibit the work of both faculty and student. Specialties of faculty members would be integrated rather than departmentalized. The integrating factor would be purpose (of each course—recognized in ministerial function). Much more could be said here—but just so much for now.

Teaching

Also, as I said, we need new teaching goals and methods. As far as teachers are concerned, it will take young men (largely), with a vision for this sort of education, to staff such a seminary. Well-seasoned professors, formed by (and conformed to) more conventional patterns, on the whole will not adapt well to this new approach. There will be some notable exceptions, of course. But not all younger men will do either; it will take flexible persons, committed fully to the basic concepts, to achieve what this program requires.

Secondly, professors should be pastorally experienced and oriented.

---

1. There would be many sections and subsections of each area.

153

They must not be men who have known nothing but the academic syndrome. Surely, one of the most serious problems seminaries have faced over the years is this gravitation of men who have no love for the pastoral ministry into seminary instruction.

Thirdly, the professors who are acquired for this new program should become models of what they teach—not merely models of someone talking about it. The discipleship methods (demonstration of theory; not theory in the abstract) *must* replace the Greek academic method (from the "academy"). Teaching, biblically speaking, is not merely *thinking* like one's teacher, but *becoming* like him (Luke 6:40). Discipleship is not an option; it is essential. It has an intratrinitarian base according to John 3, 5, 8, etc. Jesus *did* what He *saw* the Father *do* and *spoke* what He *heard* the Father *say*. If we keep His words, we will be His disciples as He is the disciple (apprentice) of His Father. Modeling is the discipleship method; showing (incarnated in a person doing it) what one speaks about.

Take, for example, exegesis. It is possible in any number of ways, for a student not only to learn the principles of exegesis (through reading and lectures), and to receive the results of his teacher's own exegesis. He also ought to be able to look over the teacher's shoulder to observe him *doing* exegesis. Then—in time—the professor ought to be able to look over the student's shoulder too. Observation and supervision, questioning an expert in action, and guiding and correcting a beginner who is making his first efforts are essential elements of good discipleship teaching. What I have suggested for exegesis should happen also across the board for *every* subject.

Now, a few random words about teaching. What should be in view is competence in ministry—not grades in courses. The emphasis on grades in our schools has not had a salutary effect on students. There must be evaluation, of course, but I'll say a word about that in a minute. When we think about students with a B+ or C− mentality, something is drastically wrong. By emphasizing grades, schools have fostered fierce competition rather than loving cooperation. Students have been encouraged to work for grades rather than for understanding, retention, and competence. They have learned how to second-guess teachers' testing styles rather than learn information, lifestyles, and skills that will be important to ministry. What we want are competent ministers; what we get are test whizzers.

Criteria for competence ought to be established, of course. The faculty *must* give much though to this. But, along these lines, at least one thing seems clear: a student must not be allowed to move on to the next learning opportunity until he becomes competent in what it is he must know, be, and do in order to assume that new responsibility for ministry. In other words, each competence must lay a foundation for the next. And, in evaluating competence, a significant part also ought to come from persons to whom he ministers—not merely from professors.

In gathering a faculty of the sort described above, there will be both opportunities and problems. At first, such a faculty will be built of younger men (for the most part), as I have said. They will be learning and earning degrees. They will not be well known. But what they do can be supplemented from video-taped materials by more conventionally oriented professors during the transition period.

Now, many questions arise. I would like to have taken more space to develop this article more fully, but this will have to do for the time being. I hope, however, that what I have written will stir some of you to thought and action. There is much at stake here; the time is late. I don't have all the answers, but I have given you a few—along with some general direction. Is there someone to whom you ought to speak about this matter, pastor? If so, make an appointment today!

65908